ECONOMIC ISSUES, PROBLEMS AND PERSPECTIVES

INCOME DISTRIBUTION IN THE UNITED STATES

MEASURES, TRENDS AND ANALYSES

ECONOMIC ISSUES, PROBLEMS AND PERSPECTIVES

Additional books in this series can be found on Nova's website under the Series tab.

Additional e-books in this series can be found on Nova's website under the e-book tab.

ECONOMIC ISSUES, PROBLEMS AND PERSPECTIVES

INCOME DISTRIBUTION IN THE UNITED STATES

MEASURES, TRENDS AND ANALYSES

CLAYTON DIAZ
EDITOR

nova publishers
New York

NOTICE TO THE READER

Library of Congress Cataloging-in-Publication Data

ISBN: 978-1-63482-675-4

Published by Nova Science Publishers, Inc. † New York

CONTENTS

PREFACE

This book also examines changes over time and across countries in the shape of the income distribution to afford Members of Congress a broader perspective when deliberating such policy issues as the progressivity of income tax rates, the generosity of social insurance programs, and the level of the minimum wage.

Chapter 1 - The distribution of income in the United States features heavily in congressional discussions about the middle class, program funding and effectiveness, new and existing target groups, government tax revenue, and social mobility, among other topics. Recently, the level and distribution of U.S. income have also been raised in the context of broader macroeconomic issues, such as economic growth. Accordingly, Congress has sought information on the absolute and relative experience of U.S. households, the range of incomes, and their dispersion.

Describing the income distribution involves several important choices about the definition of income and the level at which income data are examined. Income can be constructed narrowly (e.g., earnings only) or broadly (e.g., as the sum of earnings, capital gains, government transfers, and other sources); it can be presented in pre-tax status or reflect taxes paid and tax credits received. Income can be presented at the individual level or represent pooled resources among households, families, or tax units. These choices about how to define income affect the magnitude of income indicators and the shape and range of the U.S. income distribution. For this reason, disagreement over the interpretation of income levels and trends frequently centers on how income is defined.

This report is a guide to various measures, indicators, and graphics commonly used to describe the U.S. income distribution. It examines the complexities of income measurement, outlines important definitional and data considerations to bear in mind when using and interpreting income statistics, and reviews descriptive statistics commonly used in analysis. It also discusses the Gini index, a popular summary measure of income dispersion and an appendix presents information on additional summary indicators of income dispersion reported annually by the U.S. Census Bureau.

The report provides descriptive analysis of the U.S. income distribution to illustrate various concepts and data presentation strategies. This analysis reveals broad trends, but does not provide an exhaustive study of the distribution of income in the United States. Importantly, the report does not explore potential drivers and impacts of changes to the shape and span of the distribution.

Chapter 2 - Although not itself a subject of legislation, the shape of the income distribution enters Congress's decision-making process concerning such policy issues as taxes, means-tested benefits, and social insurance programs. Congress also considers legislation specifically in the name of those in the middle class, which is variously defined as some income level or income range within the distribution of U.S. households with income. After briefly analyzing the distribution of household money income in 2012, the report attempts to put the term "middle class" into greater perspective.

The first key point of the report is that, although there are a variety of ways to describe the income distribution, all show that income is concentrated among high-income households. Of the 122,459,000 households with income in 2012, 2.3% had incomes of at least $250,000. (The Census Bureau does not disaggregate income within the $250,000-or-more income class.) In addition, a large share of total money income accrues to those at the upper end of the distribution. In 2012, the top 5% of U.S. households with income accounted for 22.3% of total income, and the top 20% of households (which includes the top 5%) had 51.0% of all money income. A broader definition of household income, incorporating capital gains, the value of non-cash benefits (e.g., Food Stamps, Medicare and Medicaid, and employer paid health insurance), and subtracting estimates of federal taxes, tends to make the income distribution slightly more equal.

The second major point is that there is no official government definition of who belongs to the middle class, and the term means different things to different people. The middle class may refer to a group with a common point of view or to those having similar incomes, for example.

Third, absolute income appears to partly determine who belongs to the middle class. By combining money income data from the latest Annual Social and Economic Supplement to the Current Population Survey with results from surveys that asked people to identify their social class, the middle class may refer to households with income levels in 2012 that ranged from $39,736 (the bottom of the middle quintile, 20%, of households) and extended into the top quintile (households with income of $104,087 or more)—perhaps including households with incomes somewhat over $200,000.

Last, relative income may also be a defining characteristic of the middle class. In other words, the middle class appears to identify itself relative to the income of a reference group (e.g., their neighbors or coworkers). According to studies of self-reported well-being, those who constitute the middle class seemingly are of like minds with regard to their economic situation. Specifically, having incomes far above those at the lower end of the income distribution generally correlates with satisfaction to the middle class, but when those at the upper end of the distribution fare much better than they do, the level of middle-class satisfaction is generally lessened.

Chapter 3 - The historically slow rebound in the labor market from the 2007-2009 recession appears to be partly responsible for the current focus of some within the public policy community on the unequal distribution of the benefits of economic growth (e.g., higher national income) across U.S. households. This report examines changes over time and across countries in the shape of the income distribution to afford Members of Congress a broader perspective when deliberating such policy issues as the progressivity of income tax rates, the generosity of social insurance programs, and the level of the minimum wage.

Chapter 4 - In 2011, according to the Congressional Budget Office's (CBO's) estimates, average household market income— a comprehensive income measure that consists of labor income, business income, capital income (including capital gains), and retirement income—was approximately $81,000. Government transfers, which include benefits from programs such as Social Security, Medicare, and unemployment insurance, averaged approximately $13,000 per household. The sum of those two amounts, which equals before-tax income, was about $94,000, on average. Federal taxes as examined in this report comprise four separate sources: individual income taxes, payroll (or social insurance) taxes, corporate income taxes, and excise taxes. Taken together, those taxes were about $17,000 per household, on average, in 2011. Thus, average household income after taxes was about $77,000, and the average federal tax rate (federal taxes divided by before-tax income) was 17.6 percent.

In: Income Distribution in the United States
Editor: Clayton Diaz
ISBN: 978-1-63482-675-4

Chapter 1

A GUIDE TO DESCRIBING THE INCOME DISTRIBUTION*

Sarah A. Donovan

SUMMARY

The distribution of income in the United States features heavily in congressional discussions about the middle class, program funding and effectiveness, new and existing target groups, government tax revenue, and social mobility, among other topics. Recently, the level and distribution of U.S. income have also been raised in the context of broader macroeconomic issues, such as economic growth. Accordingly, Congress has sought information on the absolute and relative experience of U.S. households, the range of incomes, and their dispersion.

Describing the income distribution involves several important choices about the definition of income and the level at which income data are examined. Income can be constructed narrowly (e.g., earnings only) or broadly (e.g., as the sum of earnings, capital gains, government transfers, and other sources); it can be presented in pre-tax status or reflect taxes paid and tax credits received. Income can be presented at the individual level or represent pooled resources among households, families, or tax units. These choices about how to define income affect the magnitude of income indicators and the shape and range of the U.S.

* This is an edited, reformatted and augmented version of a Congressional Research Service publication, No. R43897, dated February 5, 2015.

income distribution. For this reason, disagreement over the interpretation of income levels and trends frequently centers on how income is defined.

This report is a guide to various measures, indicators, and graphics commonly used to describe the U.S. income distribution. It examines the complexities of income measurement, outlines important definitional and data considerations to bear in mind when using and interpreting income statistics, and reviews descriptive statistics commonly used in analysis. It also discusses the Gini index, a popular summary measure of income dispersion and an appendix presents information on additional summary indicators of income dispersion reported annually by the U.S. Census Bureau.

The report provides descriptive analysis of the U.S. income distribution to illustrate various concepts and data presentation strategies. This analysis reveals broad trends, but does not provide an exhaustive study of the distribution of income in the United States. Importantly, the report does not explore potential drivers and impacts of changes to the shape and span of the distribution.

Census data show a gap in income between households at the top of the distribution and those in the middle and bottom of the distribution. In 2013, household income at the 90th percentile was $150,000, whereas household income at the 10th percentile was $12,401. Said another way, household income at the 90th percentile was 12.1 times the level of household income at the 10th percentile. Median household income in 2013 was $51,939, up from $49,594 in 1993 (in 2013 dollars).

Census data reveal growing concentration of income at the top of the distribution between 1993 and 2013. Households in the top 20% of the distribution earned 51% of total household income in 2013, compared to 48.9% in 1993 (an increase of 4.3%). The share of total income among the bottom 20% of households was 3.2% in 2013 and 3.6% in 1993 (a decrease of 11.1%). In addition, Census calculations indicate that the Gini index increased from 0.454 in 1993 to 0.476 in 2013, indicating increased dispersion of household income.

INTRODUCTION

The distribution of income in the United States features heavily in congressional discussions about the middle class, program funding and effectiveness, new and existing target groups, government tax revenue, and social mobility, among other topics. Recently, the level and distribution of U.S. income have also been raised in the context of broader macroeconomic issues, such as economic growth.

Recent congressional activity—committee hearings and reports, communication with major media outlets, and policy research discussions about income—reveals a heightened interest among some Members in the distribution of U.S. income. This report responds to that interest by providing a guide to various measures, indicators, and graphics commonly used to describe the U.S. income distribution.[1]

This report provides descriptive analysis of the U.S. income distribution to illustrate various concepts. This analysis reveals broad trends, but does not provide an exhaustive study of the distribution of income in the United States. Importantly, the report does not explore potential drivers and impacts of changes to the shape and span of the distribution.

This report is organized as follows: first, it examines the complexities of income measurement and important definitional and data considerations to bear in mind when using and interpreting income statistics. Next, it describes two popular data sources used to study the U.S. income distribution, followed by sections on statistics commonly used to provide point-in-time analysis and to compare U.S. income across groups, time, and location. The report concludes with an explanation of the Gini index. An appendix presents information on the set of summary indicators of income dispersion reported annually by the U.S. Census Bureau.

MEASURING INCOME

On the surface, measuring income is a simple concept.[2] In practice, however, empirical analysis of the income distribution involves several choices about how income is defined and the level at which income data are examined. Income can be constructed narrowly (e.g., earnings only) or broadly (e.g., as the sum of earnings, capital gains, government transfers, and other sources). It can be presented in pre-tax status or reflect the taxes paid and tax credits received. Income can be measured at the individual level or represent pooled resources among households, families, or tax units.

These choices about how to define and organize income are consequential, because the same data can present different pictures of the income distribution depending on how income is constructed.[3] Among commonly used income definitions, movement from one income measure to another is unlikely to shift household rankings dramatically—that is, the poor are not likely to be characterized as rich, or vice versa—but poor households might not look quite as poor when the value of government transfers are included, and the level and movement in incomes at the top of the distribution will depend importantly on whether and how capital gains and personal income taxes are included. The level of income analysis—that is, whether income is measured at the individual, household, or family level—will also impact indicators used to characterize the income distribution. For example, average individual income will lie below average household income, simply because households can have multiple earners. For these reasons, disagreement over the interpretation of income levels and trends frequently centers on how income is defined.

Defining Income

Income can be seen through many lenses. It can refer simply to earnings (i.e., wages, salaries, and self-employment earnings) or to more expansive measures that span several sources of cash income and in-kind benefits and account for taxes paid and tax credits. One income formulation is not necessarily superior, as there may be valid reasons for selecting one definition over another. For example, a restrictive measure may be preferred when assessing trends and outcomes for a particular family of income streams (e.g., how market income is distributed among households). A comprehensive measure, however, may make more sense when examining households' overall ability to use income to meet basic needs. [4]

Recognizing a lack of consensus on how to define income and the benefits of definitional flexibility for certain types of analyses, the Census Bureau makes several income formulations available to data users. In addition to the money income definition it uses to produce official income dispersion estimates, Census provides annual estimates of market income, post-social insurance income, disposable income, and an income measure recommended by the National Academies of Science. Census also allows data users to customize an income measure for certain statistics by specifying which of the 42 Census income components to include.[5]

Table 1 compares three Census-defined income measures and illustrates the variability of income concepts. The first column shows money income, the income definition used by Census to calculate annual income dispersion estimates. Money income represents pre-tax cash income received on a usual basis by households; notably, it excludes occasional income such as capital gains (and losses) and in-kind benefits. Market income (second column) is a somewhat narrower concept that reflects pre-tax income from market sources. Disposable income (column three) is the most expansive formulation in the table. In addition to all components in money and market income, it includes receipt of the Earned Income Tax Credit (EITC); Supplemental Nutritional Assistance Program (SNAP); free, reduced, and regular-price school lunches; public housing and rental subsidies; and economic stimulus payments (in 2009 only) and recovery payments (in 2010 only). It deducts federal and state income taxes that remain after receipt of refundable tax credits, payroll taxes, and property-taxes on owner-occupied housing.

Defining Income: Three Areas of Special Consideration

Table 1 highlights a few points that arise regularly in research and policy discussions around the U.S. income distribution. These include whether and how to account for capital gains and losses, tax deductions and credits, and government-supported health insurance. How these components are treated is consequential for income distribution analysis because they are experienced differently by low-, middle-, and high-income individuals and households. This means the difference between including these components in income and not including them in income is not a mere shift in the distribution, but potentially alters the shares of total income held by various income groups, and where an individual or household ranks in the distribution.

Accounting for Capital Gains and Losses

One notable difference between the Census money income concept and the two alternative definitions presented in **Table 1** is the treatment of capital gains.[6] Money income, the definition used by Census to generate its annual income dispersion statistics, does not include capital gains and losses at all. This is frequently identified as a limitation of official Census income statistics in accurately characterizing U.S. income levels, distribution, and trends, because capital gains can be a significant source of income, particularly among households at the upper end of the distribution.[7]

The Internal Revenue Service (IRS) income tax return data record capital gains only when the gains are realized and reported as part of taxable income. For these data, capital gains may therefore be more visible among high-income households because they are more likely to hold (and sell) assets that produce taxable income. In addition, some contend that the standard onetime valuation of capital gains income in the year of realization (i.e., sale of asset) is misleading.[8]

This is because the value of assets can accrue over the course of several years, contributing incrementally to available resources. The counter perspective is that continuous accounting for capital gains is a purely theoretical exercise, noting that (1) living standards do not rise with asset value accrual, and (2) the view that available resources rise with asset appreciation rests on the assumption that households can obtain peak prices for their assets.[9]

Pre-tax versus Post-tax Income

The treatment of taxes (i.e., payments and credits) is another point of consideration highlighted in **Table 1**. Unlike money income and market income, disposable income presents income in post-tax status, taking into account payment of personal income taxes and receipt of tax credits. It could be argued that this income formulation provides a more realistic representation of income available for consumption in a given year. It also affects the measurement of the income distribution because tax payments and credits are likely to be experienced differently by lower- and higher-income groups. Some low-income individuals and households may not meet the earnings threshold for taxable income or otherwise have a disproportionately lower tax bill than their middle- and high-income counterparts. Likewise, low-income individuals and households are more likely to qualify for certain tax credits, such as the EITC. For these reasons, post-tax income formulations are likely to raise incomes among low-earners and reduce incomes among high-earners when compared with similar pre-tax income definitions.[10]

The Value of Government-Supported Health Insurance

The value of government-supported health insurance—such as Medicare and Medicaid—is a facet of income that is not reflected in any of the Census income definitions summarized in **Table 1**. Given its potentially sizable impact on the availability of household resources, income estimates that do not account for government health insurance have been criticized for providing a misleading picture of the income distribution. One concern is that some government-supported health benefits (e.g., Medicaid) are received disproportionately by lower-income individuals and households. Excluding this component may therefore understate the full value of resources among the low-earner group relative to those in the middle and top of the distribution.[11]

Table 1. Three U.S. Census Bureau Household Income Definitions

	Money Income	Market Income	Disposable Income
Income Components			
Earnings (wages, salaries, and self-employment income)	x	x	x
Interest income	x	x	x
Dividend income	x	x	x
Rents, royalties, estate, and trust income	x	x	x
Nongovernment retirement pensions and annuities	x	x	x
Nongovernment survivor pensions and annuities	x	x	x
Nongovernment disability pensions and annuities	x	x	x
Realized capital gains		x[a]	x[a]
Social Security	x		x
Unemployment compensation	x		x
Workers' compensation	x		x
Veterans' payments other than pensions	x		x
Government retirement pensions and annuities	x		x
Government survivor pensions and annuities	x		x
Government disability pensions and annuities	x		x
Public assistance (includes TANF and other cash welfare)	x		x
Supplemental Security Income	x		x
Veterans' pensions	x		x
Federal earned income credit			x
Government educational assistance	x		x
Nongovernment educational assistance	x	x	x
Supplemental Nutritional Assistance Program			x
Free and reduced-price school lunches			x
Public housing and rental subsidies			x
Child Support	x	x	x
Alimony	x	x	x
Regular contributions from persons not living in the household	x	x	x
Money income not elsewhere classified	x	x	x

Table 1. (Continued)

	Money Income	Market Income	Disposable Income
Imputed return to home equity on owner-occupied housing		x	x
Regular-price school lunches			x
Economic stimulus payments (2009 ASEC only)			x
Economic recovery payments (2010 ASEC only)			x
Deducted from Income			
Realized capital losses		x[a]	x[a]
Federal income taxes after refundable credits except EIC			x
State income taxes after all refundable credits			x
Payroll taxes (FICA and other mandatory deductions)			x
Property taxes on owner-occupied housing			x
Work-related expenses excluding child care		x	x

Source: Table prepared by the Congressional Research Service (CRS) using U.S Census Bureau definitions, available at http://www.census.gov/cps/data /incdef.html.

a. The last year for which capital gains and losses estimates are available from the Census Bureau is 2007 (data collected in 2008).

How Definitions Affect the Income Distribution: An Illustration

Figure 1 presents the percentage of U.S. households with no income in 2007 (left side) and the percentage of households that earned $100,000 or more in 2007 (right side), when the three definitions in **Table 1** are applied to Census data. The data year 2007 was selected for **Figure 1** because that is the last year that Census produced estimates for capital gains and losses (see footnote 6).

When the most restrictive measure—market income—is applied, Census estimates show that 4.0% of households had zero income in 2007. This measure falls to 1.2% when the money income definition is applied, reflecting the value of government cash transfers on incomes at the bottom of the distribution. The disposable income definition, which takes a fuller range of government benefits and federal and state taxes (payments and credits) into account, produces the fewest no-income households (0.5%).

Movement from the most restrictive income definition (market income) to the most expansive income definition (disposable income) produced a smaller and smaller number of households with no income in 2007; that is, it appears to raise incomes at the bottom of the distribution. The opposite pattern is observed at the top of the distribution: the addition of income dimensions to the income definition appears to reduce the number of households with high incomes. The market income and money income definitions produce nearly identical percentages of households with $100,000 or more in 2007 (20.4% and 20.3%, respectively). The group of high-earning households is smallest at 11.8%, when the broadest definition, disposable income, is used.

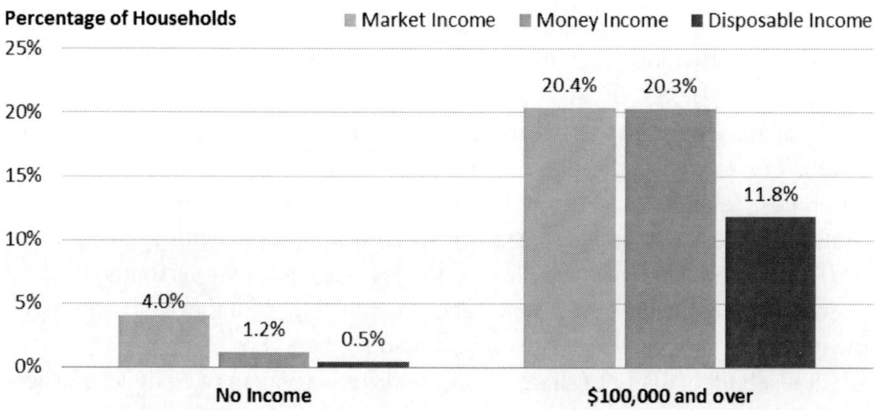

Source: Figure created by the Congressional Research Service (CRS) using data from the U.S. Census Bureau CPS Table Creator, available at http://www.census.gov /cps/data/cpstablecreator.html.

Figure 1. Households at the Bottom and Top of the Distribution for Three Census Definitions of Household Income, 2007.

Level of Analysis

Income can be presented at the individual level or represent pooled resources among families, households, or tax units. Although synonymous in regular discourse, family and household concepts can have important distinctions for statistical purposes. The Census Bureau defines a family as two or more people with a direct familial relationship (i.e., related by birth, marriage, or adoption), and a household as one or more people who live together and may or may not be related. A household may be a single person, a collection of roommates, or one or more families living together. Tax units are an IRS concept and describe the person or persons filing a tax return (i.e., individual filer and dependents or married filers and their dependents). A tax unit can represent an individual, an entire household or family, or several tax units can reside within a household or family.

The income distribution will look different depending on whether it is organized at the individual level or household (or other aggregate) level. Individuals (and single tax units) are more numerous and have lower average income levels than households and families, because the latter groups can have multiple earners. Individual income analysis will reveal more low-income persons—such as college students with summer jobs—who are otherwise aggregated into household or family income measures. For these reasons, income analyses that organize income at the individual level are not directly comparable with those that use data on multi-member units that may pool resources.

Comparability issues affect income data organized at multi-member levels as well. For example, the number of members can vary considerably across households, families, and tax units, complicating comparisons of per-person resources. That is, a member of a four-person household with an income of $52,000 does not have the same access to resources as a two-person household earning $52,000 in the same year. The composition of units also matters to how resources are pooled and shared across members. For example, a mother-child household is likely to share resources differently than two adult unrelated roommates. Some researchers and organizations adjust data in response to these issues.[12]

INCOME DATA

The potential for meaningful income distribution analysis rests on the quality and coverage of the underlying data. Government sources often offer the best option, given the scale of effort, cost, and sensitive nature of collecting income information.[13] Census Bureau household survey data and IRS tax return administrative data are two main sources of annual data used to characterize and study the U.S. income distribution.[14] Both agencies publish official statistics on an annual basis and offer some public access—with restrictions—to the individual records. Census and IRS data have relative strengths and important individual limitations that affect their potential to fully characterize the U.S. income distribution.[15]

Census Data

The U.S. Census Bureau collects income data annually from a random sample of households through the Current Population Survey (CPS) Annual Social and Economic Supplement (ASEC). Data are collected from February to April of each year and measure income from the previous calendar year.[16] Census compiles official income statistics based on these data and publishes them in the annual *Income and Poverty in the United States* report.[17]

Census reports statistics on money income, which represents pre-tax cash income received by households on a regular basis from market and nonmarket sources. In addition to regular market income, money income as defined by Census includes the value of all public cash transfers (e.g., Temporary Assistance for Needy Families [TANF]). It excludes periodic income, such as capital gains, and in-kind transfers (e.g., Supplemental Nutritional Assistance Program [SNAP] benefits and employer contributions to health insurance plans). (See **Table 1**.)

Some aspects of the Census Bureau CPS-ASEC data limit its usefulness in characterizing households at the top of the distribution. To start, Census income estimates are based on information collected from a random sample of households; survey responses are extrapolated to population estimates using sample weights. This method tends to be most effective for estimating the level and distribution of income among middle- and low-income households, where households are clustered together and income ranges are relatively narrow. Estimates at the top, however, where incomes are spread much farther apart, can be quite sensitive to sample composition.

Data recording and internal processing procedures introduce further restrictions on top incomes in the CPS-ASEC data.[18] Census limits the number of digits available to survey interviewers when recording individual responses to income questions, effectively capping the level of income that can be reported. This limit was raised from $299,999 to $9,999,999 for each of the four earned-income sources in 1994, when Census moved from a pen-and-paper data collection method to a computer-assisted interview.[19] This means that during the interview, if an individual reports earned income of $10 million or more, it will be recorded by the enumerator as $9,999,999. Once collected, Census edits its income data to minimize the incidence of interviewer error or misreporting on the part of the individual interviewed. For the purposes of Census-published data tabulations and public-use data, the internal processing limit is $999,999 for each of the four individual earnings categories.[20] Finally, Census has historically faced problems in capturing accurate information on interest and dividend income, which is disproportionately received by high-income households.[21]

In addition, the CPS-ASEC survey has undergone several methodological changes that compromise comparability of income estimates over time. These include the periodic update of Census weights, the addition of new income categories, and changes in recording limits. The Census Bureau is careful to note these changes for published statistics in detailed table footnotes.

IRS Records

IRS records capture information on pre-tax, pre-transfer taxable income from a large sample of households, and are viewed as a superior data source for examining the top of the income distribution. Unlike the Census CPS-ASEC, IRS data are based on administrative records (i.e., tax returns filed by tax units) and do not represent a random sample. IRS systematically collects data on taxable income from all individuals who are required to file. Its sample is therefore individuals (or units) with taxable income who comply with federal tax law.

IRS data provide a better view of incomes at the top, because this group is almost universally required to file.[22] However, it has less coverage among low-income individuals and households since some low-income individuals and families are not required to file tax returns at all. It may also undercount income received by this group because certain types of government assistance provided predominantly to lower-income households are not reported on federal tax returns (e.g., SSI and TANF payments). In addition, the types of capital gains realized most often by middle- and lower-income filers tend to be untaxed (e.g., from sale of residential property) and therefore unreported on tax returns.

IRS data also do not offer perfect comparability over time. Changes to the federal tax code affect how income is reported (e.g., as personal versus business income), the types of income that are taxable, and who is required to file. Tax code changes can also stimulate household behavior with consequences for taxable income. This may include the strategic sell off of assets in anticipation of higher capital gains taxes.[23] It may also affect labor supply decisions, and hence earnings, although the literature offers no clear guidance on how labor supply responds to tax code changes in practice.[24]

DATA USED IN THIS REPORT

Analyses in subsequent sections of this report employ U.S. Census Bureau statistics on household money income, collected through the CPS-ASEC and published annually in the Census Bureau report *Income and Poverty in the United States*.[25] The exception is Appendix **Figure A-1**, which shows data compiled by the Congressional Budget Office (CBO). The Census definition of money income describes regular, pre-tax cash income from market and nonmarket sources. It excludes capital gains and in-kind forms of income (e.g., noncash government benefits, goods produced and consumed at home or farm, employer contributions). Income is observed and described at the household level.

Data for 2013 are used to illustrate point-in-time measures.[26] When indicators are considered over time, the report uses the time period 1993-2013. The base year for time series comparisons is set to 1993 because significant methodological changes affect the comparability of Census income measures before and after 1993.

All data are reported in 2013 dollars. Income levels from 1993 to 2012 are adjusted (by Census) using the Consumer Price Index Research Series using Current Methods (CPI-U-RS),which applies various methodological improvements to the Bureau of Labor Statistics (BLS) Consumer Price Index for all Urban Consumers (CPI-U).[27]

DESCRIBING A DISTRIBUTION: THE BASICS

Even in their simplest forms, descriptive statistics can provide insight to the income of the "typical" household and characterize the full spread of incomes, offering a meaningful starting point to policy discussions about household income.

Describing the Typical Household

The mean and median are the main measures used to describe the center of a distribution and are prime candidates for describing the experience of the typical household. Mean income is obtained by dividing total aggregate household income by the total number of households, that is, the simple average or the level of income that each household would have in hand if total income were distributed equally. It is particularly useful as a measure of central tendency when the distribution is symmetrical, but loses power as a measure of the typical household's income when the distribution is skewed and in the presence of outliers.[28]

The median is generally viewed as a better indicator of typical household income. It is the level of income that divides the population into two equal-sized groups: the lowest 50% of households (who earn less than the median value of income) and the top 50% of households (who earn more than the median value of income). For example, the Census Bureau estimates that median household income in the United States was $51,939 in 2013. This means that in 2013, approximately 50% of households had incomes above $51,939 and 50% of households earned less than $51,939. For reference, mean household income was $72,641 in 2013.

To see the relative merits of the median as a measure of the typical household, consider the following example. Ten households line a street, each with an annual income of $52,000. Median and mean annual household income are therefore both $52,000 for this street. On January 1 of the next year, the 10th house wins the lottery, paid through an annuity that raises its annual income to $200,000. In an instant, mean household income for this street has increased from $52,000 to $66,800, while the median remains $52,000. Despite this increase in mean household income, the situation of 90% of households is unchanged, because households on this street do not pool resources. Instead the median conveys more accurate information on typical household income for this population.

Characterizing the Breadth and Shape of the Distribution

Information on breadth of earnings and the placement and concentration of households along the income spectrum is interesting from a policy perspective. The distributional range, the difference between the highest and lowest value, is arguably the simplest measure of dispersion. In terms of household income, it is the difference between the income of the richest household and income of the poorest household.[29] Despite the simplicity of the indictor, data collection methods and statutory privacy rules make calculating the range nearly impossible. Consequently, no official data are publicly available on the absolute highest and lowest income households in the United States. See **Appendix A** for a discussion of incomes at the top of the distribution.

The shape of the income distribution reveals how households line up and cluster along the spectrum of incomes. The shape of a distribution can be described as symmetric, right-skewed or left-skewed. Symmetric distributions (**Figure 2**, Panel A) are balanced, with the center of the data in the center of the graph. Because the "tails" of the distribution (i.e., the few households at the very top and very bottom of the distribution) balance each other out, the mean and median values are identical or very close to each other. Skewed distributions are asymmetric and characterized by a mass of observations (e.g., households) to one side of the graph with either a long or thick tail to the other side. When the mass of households are found clustered toward the bottom of the distribution, with a tail to the right, the distribution is said to be right-skewed or positively skewed (**Figure 2**, Panel B). The group of relatively high incomes at the top pulls up the mean, so that it will exceed the median in right-skewed distributions. The distribution is left-skewed or negatively skewed when mass is concentrated among high values, with the tail leading to the left (**Figure 2**, Panel C). The mean in left-skewed distributions is pulled down by the relatively low-income households that form its tail, and it will lie below the median. Income distributions are typically right-skewed.

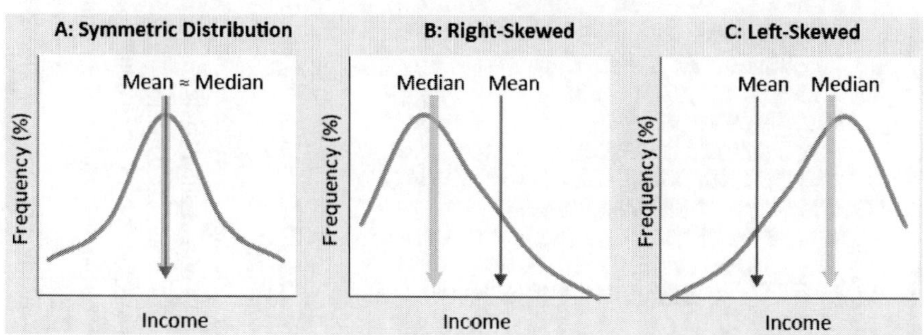

Source: CRS.

Figure 2. Symmetric and Skewed Distributions.

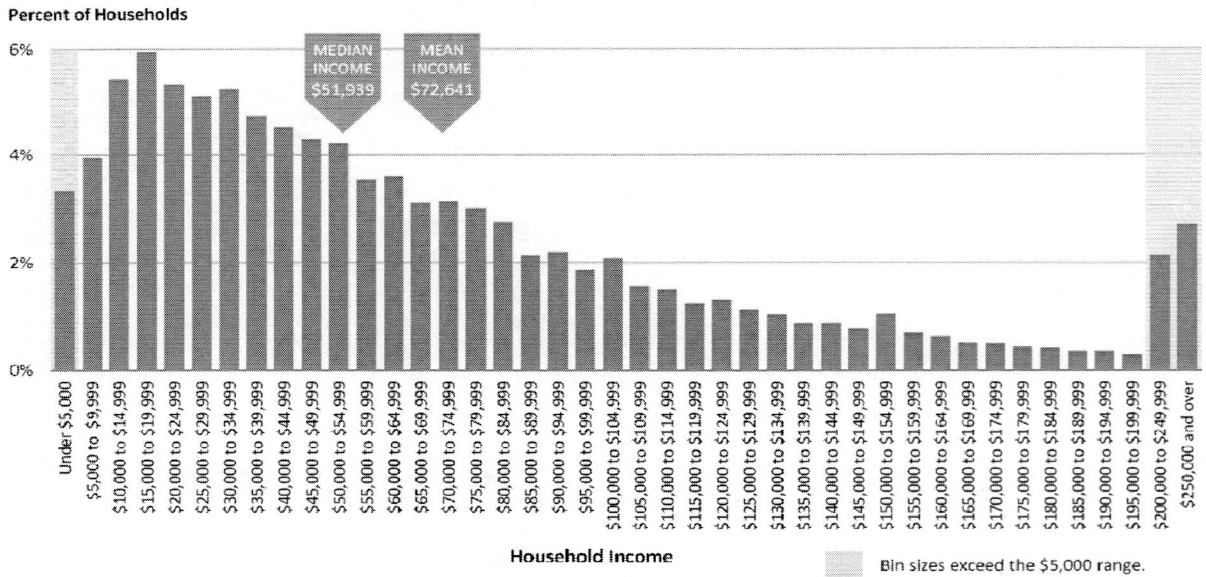

Source: U.S. Census Bureau, Annual Social and Economic Supplement, available at http://www.census.gov/hhes/www/cpstables/032014/hhinc/toc.htm.

Notes: Income in this figure refers to household *money income* as defined by the Census Bureau: pre-tax cash income received by households on a regular basis from market and nonmarket sources. Money income excludes periodic income, such as capital gains, and in-kind transfers. Due to the way the Census Bureau aggregates incomes at the top of the distribution, the top two income groups—"$200,000 to $249,000" and "$250,000 and over"—represent wider income ranges than the groups that categorize the majority of the distribution. The "Under $5,000" group includes households earning zero or negative money income.

Figure 3. Distribution of Household Income, 2013.

The Frequency Distribution

Graphical representations of an income distribution, such as the frequency distribution in **Figure 3**, can convey information about central tendency (mean and median), shape, and range in a concise and intuitive way. **Figure 3** shows the distribution of U.S. household income in 2013. It plots income levels on the horizontal axis and the percentage of households on the vertical axis, and shows a right-skewed distribution. In 2013, median household income was $51,939 and average household income was $72,641.

As noted earlier, Census does not provide a lot of detail on the income levels and the distribution of high-income households. This is reflected in **Figure 3**, which divides U.S. households into several income "bins" based on their money income in 2013. Between $5,000 and $199,999, incomes are grouped in bins with a $5,000 range. At $200,000, the scale changes: the penultimate bin has a range of $200,000 to $249,999 and the final bin includes all incomes at $250,000 and over. The first bin (under $5,000) has a range in excess of $5,000 because it includes negative income values.[30]

MAKING COMPARISONS

All of the indicators presented so far can be used to examine how income varies across income groups, time, or location. This type of analysis can inform discussions around changing program participation patterns, differential access to resources across groups and locations, trends in the absolute and relative experience of U.S. households, and efforts to foster social mobility.

Quantiles: Comparing Income Groups

Recent conversations about income in the United States tend to draw comparisons between income groups (e.g., top, middle, and bottom income households). Quantiles are a helpful tool for such cross-group analysis. They divide households—ordered by income from lowest to highest— into groups of equal size (i.e., equal number of households) and provide a means for defining the top, middle, and bottom of the income distribution. Once defined, incomes can be compared and contrasted across and within income groups. Commonly used quantiles include *quartiles*, which divide the population into quarters, *quintiles*, which divide the population into fifths, and *deciles* and *percentiles*, which divide the populations into tenths and hundredths, respectively.

Quantiles divide the population into groups with the same number of members (e.g., households, individuals); however, they do not necessarily divide individuals or households into equally spaced income brackets. Where households are clustered together, traditionally at the bottom and middle of the distribution, the income range for quantiles is likely to be smaller (sometimes much smaller) than the income range at the very top of the distribution, where households are spread far apart.

The Census Bureau publishes several quantile-based measures of income dispersion each year, including household income at selected percentile limits, income ratios of selected percentiles, mean income by quintile, and share of total household income held by quintiles. **Table 2** provides selected Census measures for 2013.

Income percentile limits (**Table 2**, Panel A) report the level of household income at various dividing points of the income distribution. For example, the 50th percentile limit is the level of income that divides the population in half (i.e., the median). Income at the 90th percentile limit indicates that the bottom 90% of households received less than $150,000 in 2013, while the top 10% of households received more than $150,000. A comparison of percentile limits at the 80th and 20th percentiles reveals that the 60% of households in the middle of the distribution received money income between $20,900 and $105,910 in 2013.

An income ratio (**Table 2**, Panel B) is a relative measure that expresses income at one percentile limit as a multiple (or fraction) of income at another percentile limit. For example, the $90^{th}/10^{th}$ income ratio was 12.10 in 2013. This number is calculated by dividing the household income at the 90th percentile ($150,000) by that at the 10th percentile ($12,401). It indicates that the 90th percentile household took in money income that was just over 12 times the money income received by the household at the 10th percentile.

Census reports two sets of statistics that describe household income quintiles (**Table 2**, Panel C). Quintile mean income is the average income of households within a given quintile, calculated by dividing total quintile income (i.e., the sum of all household income within a quintile) by the number of households in the quintile. As expected, quintile mean income rises throughout the distribution, with the largest jump in mean income between the 4th and 5th quintiles.

The quintile share of total income describes the percentage of total income held in aggregate by members of a given quintile. It is the ratio of *total quintile income* to *total income for all households*. In 2013, the bottom 20% of households (i.e., the lowest quintile) received 3.2% of total household money income, the middle 60% (the sum of shares for the second, third, and fourth quintiles) received 45.8%, and the top 20% of households received 51%. For reference, because each quintile represents 20% of the population of households, a 20% income share in each quintile would represent a mathematically equal distribution of household income.

Table 2. Quantile-based Measures of Household Income Dispersion, 2013

A. Household Income at Selected Percentile Limits		
10th Percentile	$12,401	
20th Percentile	$20,900	
50th Percentile (Median)	$51,939	
80th Percentile	$105,910	
90th Percentile	$150,000	
95th Percentile	$196,000	
B. Income Ratios of Selected Percentiles		
90th/10th Income Ratio	12.10	
90th/50th Income Ratio	2.89	
50th/10th Income Ratio	4.19	
C. Quintiles Incomes	Quintile Mean	Share of Total Household Income
Lowest Quintile	$11,651	3.2
Second Quintile	$30,509	8.4
Third Quintile	$52,322	14.4
Fourth Quintile	$83,519	23.0
Top Quintile	$185,206	51.0

Source: Table created by CRS based on data from U.S. Census Bureau, Current Population Survey, Annual Social and Economic Supplement, 2013, available at http://www.census.gov/hhes/www/income

Notes: Income in this table refers to household money income as defined by the Census Bureau: pre-tax cash income received by households on a regular basis from market and nonmarket sources. Money income excludes periodic income, such as capital gains, and in-kind transfers.

Trends: Making Comparisons over Time

This section provides several examples of how to present and interpret income comparisons over time. A common data source is used to calculate statistics compared over time, with minor year-to-year changes in data collection and processing methodology. However, a common source is not always available for certain comparisons. In these cases it is tremendously important to note any divergence in data source, level of data organization (e.g., household versus family), definitions, and relevant methodological chances. Without appropriate caveats, these methodological and definitional differences can be interpreted erroneously as changes (or lack of change) in actual income, and provide misleading information.

Trends in Median Income

Simple indicators like median income can be used to describe the experience of the typical household over time. **Figure 4** shows the trend in median household income between 1993 and 2013. Overall, real median household income increased from $49,594 in 1993 to $51,939 in 2013, with notable fluctuation over this period. A pattern of declining median income during periods of economic recession can be observed for the 2001 and 2007-2009 recessions. Median household income in 2013 was slightly higher than median household income in 1995 ($51,719 in 2013 dollars).

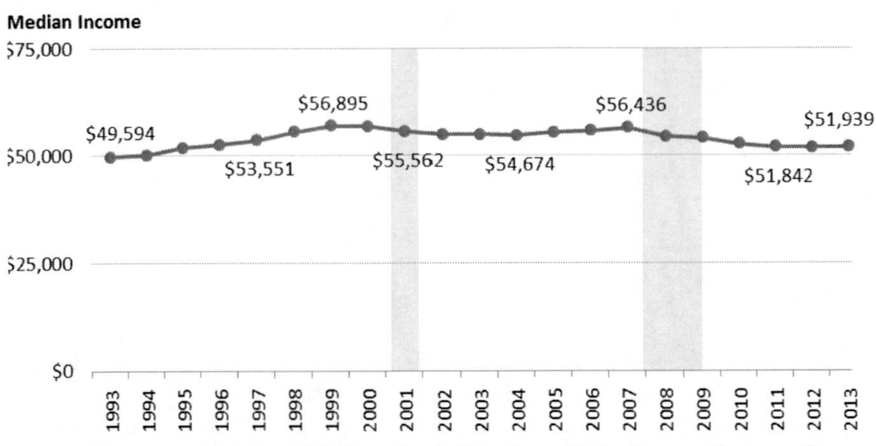

Source: Figure created by CRS based on data from U.S. Census Bureau, Current Population Survey, Annual Social and Economic Supplements, 1993-2013, available at http://www.census.gov/hhes/www/income index.html.

Notes: Income in this figure refers to household money income as defined by the Census Bureau: pre-tax cash income received by households on a regular basis from market and nonmarket sources. Money income excludes periodic income, such as capital gains, and in-kind transfers. Periods of recession are shaded in gray. Recession data are from the National Bureau of Economic Research, http://www.nber.org/cycles and reflect the 2001 recession (March 2001-November 2001) and the 2007-2009 recession (December 2007-June 2009).

Figure 4. Median Household Income, 1993-2013; (in 2013 CPI-U-RS adjusted dollars).

The Changing Shape of the Distribution: Mean-to-Median Ratio

As noted in the discussion of **Figure 2**, the shape of the distribution affects the relative position of mean and median. Drawing on this relationship, the mean-to-median ratio can be used to convey big picture information about the shape of distribution. When a distribution is symmetrical, mean and median will be the same (or very close), and the mean-to-median ratio will be one. The mean exceeds the median for a right-skewed distribution, characterized by a mass of observations on the left side of the graph and a tail to the right, yielding a mean-to-median ratio that exceeds one.[31]

Observed over time, the mean-to-median ratio provides information about the extent to which the mean is approaching or retreating from the median, and can be used to gauge changes to the shape of an income distribution. **Figure 5** plots the mean-to-median ratio from 1993 to 2013. For all years, the mean-to-median ratio is greater than one, indicating a right-skewed distribution throughout the time period. Between 1993 and 2013, both mean and median income increased in real terms (not shown in **Figure 5**), but growth in average income outpaced growth for the median.[32] This is captured by the rise in the mean-to-median income from 1.33 to 1.40. In terms of the shape of the distribution, a rising mean-to-median ratio suggests an increasingly right-skewed distribution.[33]

Quantile Analysis over Time

Quantile trend analysis can reveal changing patterns in the absolute and relative experience of U.S. households. **Figure 6** presents mean quintile household income from 1993 to 2013. A few points of interest can be taken from this graph. First, mean income among the top quintile is markedly above the other four quintiles for the duration of the observed period. In all years, mean income among the top quintile was at least twice as large as the mean income in the fourth quintile. Second, mean income increased for the 2nd, 3rd,

4th, and top quintiles over this time period—though the rate of growth in mean quintile income becomes steadily smaller when moving from the top quintile to the second quintile.[34] Finally, quintile mean income growth stalls or declines during periods of recession.

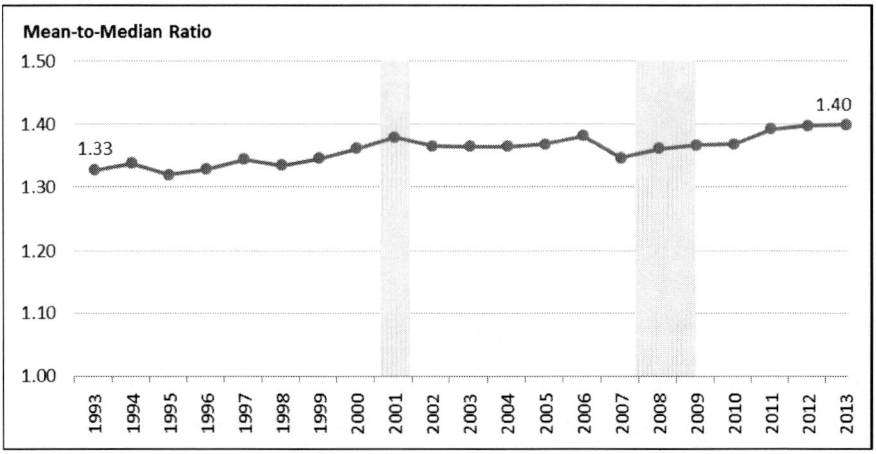

Source: Figure created by CRS based on data from U.S. Census Bureau, Current Population Survey, Annual Social and Economic Supplements, 1993-2013, available at http://www.census.gov/hhes/www/income index.html.

Notes: Income in this figure refers to household money income as defined by the Census Bureau: pre-tax cash income received by households on a regular basis from market and nonmarket sources. Money income excludes periodic income, such as capital gains, and in-kind transfers. Periods of recession are shaded in gray. Recession data are from the National Bureau of Economic Research, http://www.nber.org/cycles and reflect the 2001 recession (March 2001-November 2001) and the 2007-2009 recession (December 2007-June 2009).

Figure 5. Mean-to-Median Ratio, 1993-2013.

Figure 7 shows the evolution of 90-10, 90-50, and 50-10 income ratios between 1993 and 2013, and can be used to assess relative experiences of income groups over time. Households at the 90th, 50th, and 10th percentiles are traditional stand-ins for the top, middle, and bottom of the income distribution. Movement across these ratios, therefore, can be used to gauge changes in the relative experience of top to bottom (90-10 ratio), top to middle (90-50 ratio), and middle to bottom (50- 10 ratio). All ratios increased between 1993 and 2013, indicating that the income groups are moving farther apart from each other. The most pronounced change is in the 90-10 ratio, which increased from 10.6 to 12.1 (or approximately 14%).

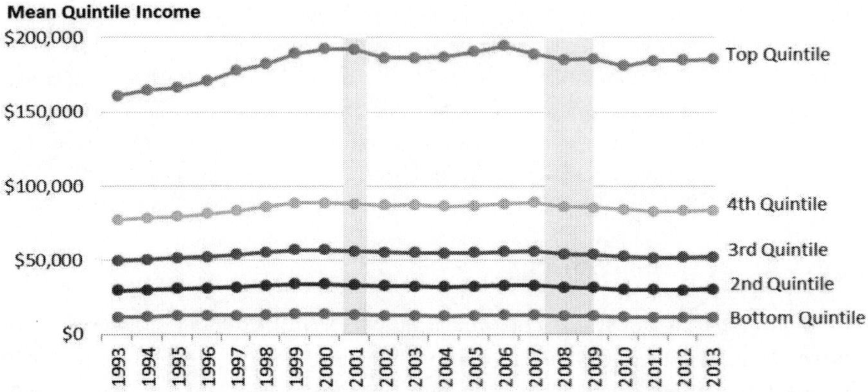

Source: Figure created by CRS based on data from U.S. Census Bureau, Current Population Survey, Annual Social and Economic Supplements, 1993-2013, available at http://www.census.gov/hhes/www/income index.html.

Notes: Income in this figure refers to household money income as defined by the Census Bureau: pre-tax cash income received by households on a regular basis from market and nonmarket sources. Money income excludes periodic income, such as capital gains, and in-kind transfers. Periods of recession are shaded in gray. Recession data are from the National Bureau of Economic Research, http://www.nber.org/cycles and reflect the 2001 recession (March 2001-November 2001) and the 2007-2009 recession (December 2007-June 2009).

Figure 6. Mean Quintile Income, 1993-2013; (in 2013 CPI-U-RS dollars).

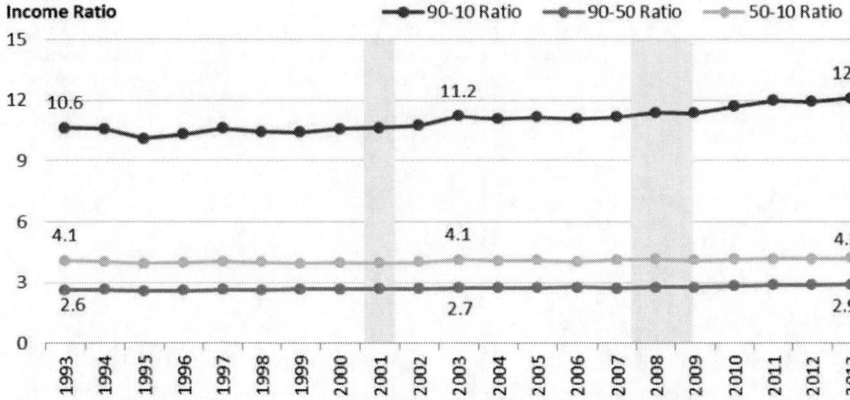

Source: Figure created by CRS based on data from U.S. Census Bureau, Current Population Survey, Annual Social and Economic Supplements, 1993-2013, available at http://www.census.gov/hhes/www/income index.html.

Notes: Income in this figure refers to household money income as defined by the Census Bureau: pre-tax cash income received by households on a regular basis from market and nonmarket sources. Money income excludes periodic income, such as capital gains, and in-kind transfers. Periods of recession are shaded in gray. Recession data are from the National Bureau of Economic Research, http://www.nber.org/cycles and reflect the 2001 recession (March 2001-November 2001) and the 2007-2009 recession (December 2007-June 2009).

Figure 7. Income Ratios, 1993-2013.

An interesting question, and one that is not immediately apparent from **Figure 7**, is whether growth in the 90-10 ratio reflects growing distance between the bottom and middle households or relatively high-income growth at the very top (i.e., a further extension of the right tail). To address this question, income ratios are sometimes expressed (and graphed) in terms of cumulative percentage change from an anchor year. **Figure 8** does just that. It converts the same data into the cumulative percentage change since 1993. All ratios show growth over their 1993 values, but more notably, the 90-50 ratio growth tracked closely with the 90-10 ratio while the 50- 10 ratio exhibits low to no growth (over the 1993 ratio). The take away from these patterns is the rise in the 90-10 ratio is driven by growth at the top half (90-50) of the distribution (i.e., the extension of the right tail).

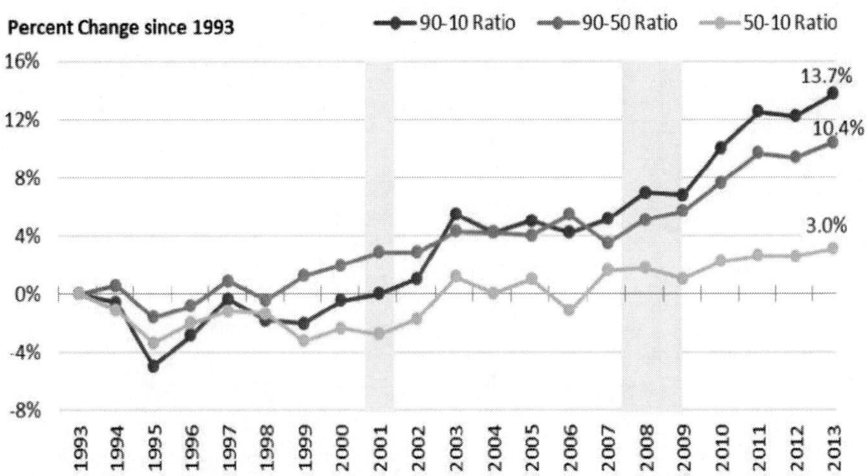

Source: Figure created by CRS based on data from U.S. Census Bureau, Current Population Survey, Annual Social and Economic Supplements, 1993-2013, available at http://www.census.gov/hhes/www/income index.html.

Notes: Income in this figure refers to household money income as defined by the Census Bureau: pre-tax cash income received by households on a regular basis from market and nonmarket sources. Money income excludes periodic income, such as capital gains, and in-kind transfers. Periods of recession are shaded in gray. Recession data are from the National Bureau of Economic Research, http://www.nber.org/cycles and reflect the 2001 recession (March 2001-November 2001) and the 2007-2009 recession (December 2007-June 2009).

Figure 8. Cumulative Percentage Change in Income Ratios, 1993-2013.

Figure 9 compares quintile income shares across 1993, 2003, and 2013, and reveals growing concentration of U.S. household income at the top of the distribution over the past 20 years. The top of the distribution held a disproportionate share of income in 1993, 2003, and 2013. The share of income among the top 20% of the distribution grew from 48.9% in 1993 to 49.8% in 2003 and to 51% in 2013. The shares of total income held by each of the four lower quintiles fell between 1993 and 2003, and again between 2003 and 2013.

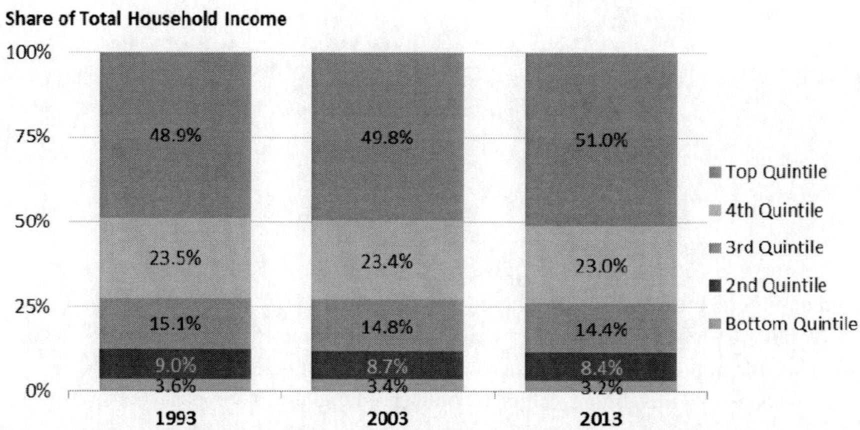

Source: Figure created by CRS based on data from U.S. Census Bureau, Current Population Survey, Annual Social and Economic Supplements, 1993-2013, available at http://www.census.gov/hhes/www/income index.html.

Notes: Income in this figure refers to household money income as defined by the Census Bureau: pre-tax cash income received by households on a regular basis from market and nonmarket sources. Money income excludes periodic income, such as capital gains, and in-kind transfers.

Figure 9. Quintile Shares of Total Income, 1993-2013.

Figure 10 translates the movement in income shares across quintiles into the percentage change in quintile share since 1993. This presentation can help identify trends and *changes* in trends. **Figure 10** suggests 2000 was a turning point of sorts for the top quintile and bottom three quintiles. Prior to 2000, each quintile fluctuated close to a 2% increase or decrease over its 1993 share. After 2000, **Figure 10** shows a relatively steady climb in the income share held by the top quintile, paired with declining shares among the bottom three quintiles; the fourth quintile continued to fluctuate steadily around a 2% cumulative change. It is important to note that data points shown in the line graphs in **Figure 10** represent cumulative change since 1993; they do not describe year-by-year (i.e., annual) percentage change (except for 1994) nor depict percentage *point* changes.

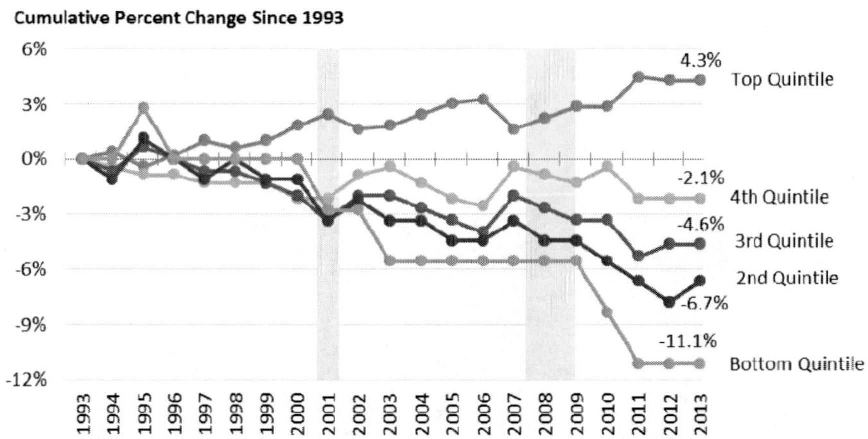

Source: Figure created by CRS based on data from U.S. Census Bureau, Current Population Survey, Annual Social and Economic Supplements, 1993-2013, available at http://www.census.gov/hhes/www/income index.html.

Notes: Income in this figure refers to household money income as defined by the Census Bureau: pre-tax cash income received by households on a regular basis from market and nonmarket sources. Money income excludes periodic income, such as capital gains, and in-kind transfers. Periods of recession are shaded in gray. Recession data are from the National Bureau of Economic Research, http://www.nber.org/cycles and reflect the 2001 recession (March 2001-November 2001) and the 2007-2009 recession (December 2007-June 2009).

Figure 10. Cumulative Change in Quintile Shares of Total Income Since 1993.

Figure 9 and **Figure 10** present the same information in visually different ways. In comparing the two charts, the decline in income share among the lower quintiles appears much more pronounced in **Figure 10**. This happens because percentage point changes (**Figure 9**) reflect an absolute change in percentage points, whereas the percentage change shown in **Figure 10** is a *relative* difference that is sensitive to base (i.e., value in 1993).[35] Since the lowest quintile has a small base (3.6% in 1993), even small absolute changes in percentage points will represent a large percentage change. For example, **Figure 10** shows an 11.1% fall in income share for the lowest quintile between 1993 and 2013, but the same change is shown in **Figure 9** as a 0.4 percentage point decrease.

Comparing Income by Geographical Location

Variation in Median Household Income across States

Comparing income statistics across U.S. states can reveal interesting economic and distributional variation that is otherwise masked by national-level data. **Figure 11** maps state median income in 2013. Some broad geo-economic patterns emerge. For example, a band of states in the southern part of the country had median income under $45,000 in 2013, while a cluster of states on the northeast coast had median incomes of $60,000 or more in the same year. This difference does not necessarily imply that median households in southern states had three-quarters or less the purchasing power of median households in coastal northeast states, because price levels are also found to fluctuate across states.

Accounting for Regional Price Variation

Income comparisons over time and location can reflect true differences in purchasing power, and they can also reflect differences in price. Adjusting time series income data for inflation is standard practice, as it is generally acknowledged that prices change over time and affect the dollar value of income. Less recognized is the potential for wide variation in prices across geographical divisions. For the United States, the Commerce Department Bureau of Economic Analysis estimates that in 2012, average price levels (for consumption goods and services) in the District of Columbia were more than 18% higher than the national price average, while prices were nearly 14% below the national average in Mississippi (See **Figure 12**).

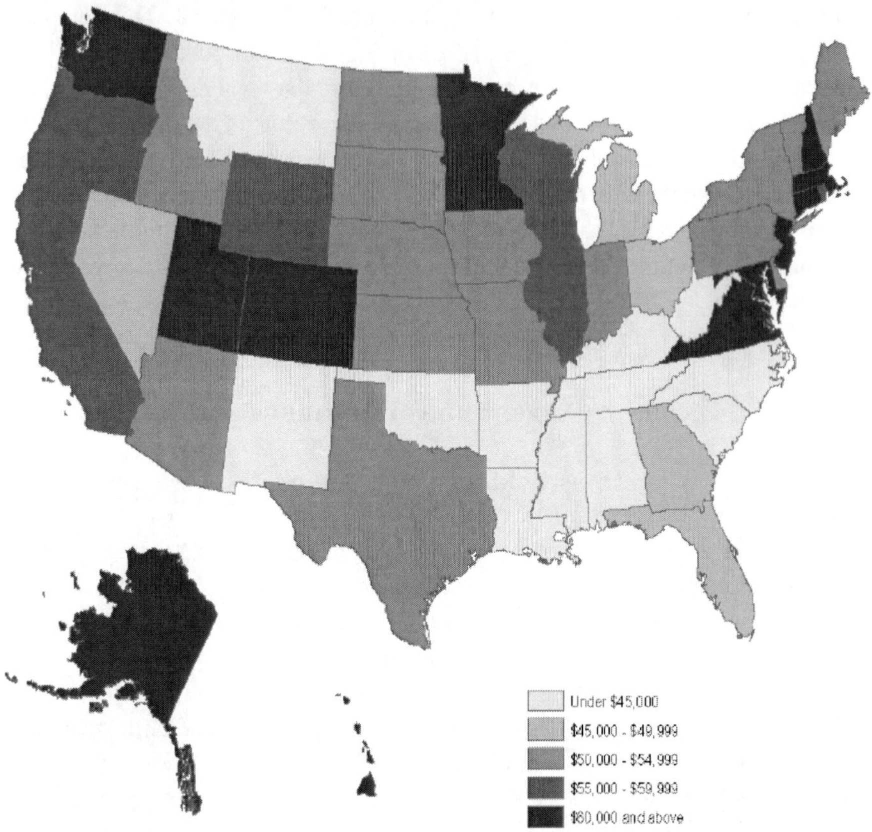

Source: Figure created CRS based on data from U.S. Census Bureau, Current Population Survey, Annual Social and Economic Supplement, 2013, available at http://www.census.gov/hhes/www/income

Notes: Income in this figure refers to household money income as defined by the Census Bureau: pre-tax cash income received by households on a regular basis from market and nonmarket sources. Money income excludes periodic income, such as capital gains, and in-kind transfers.

Figure 11. Median Household Income by State, 2013.

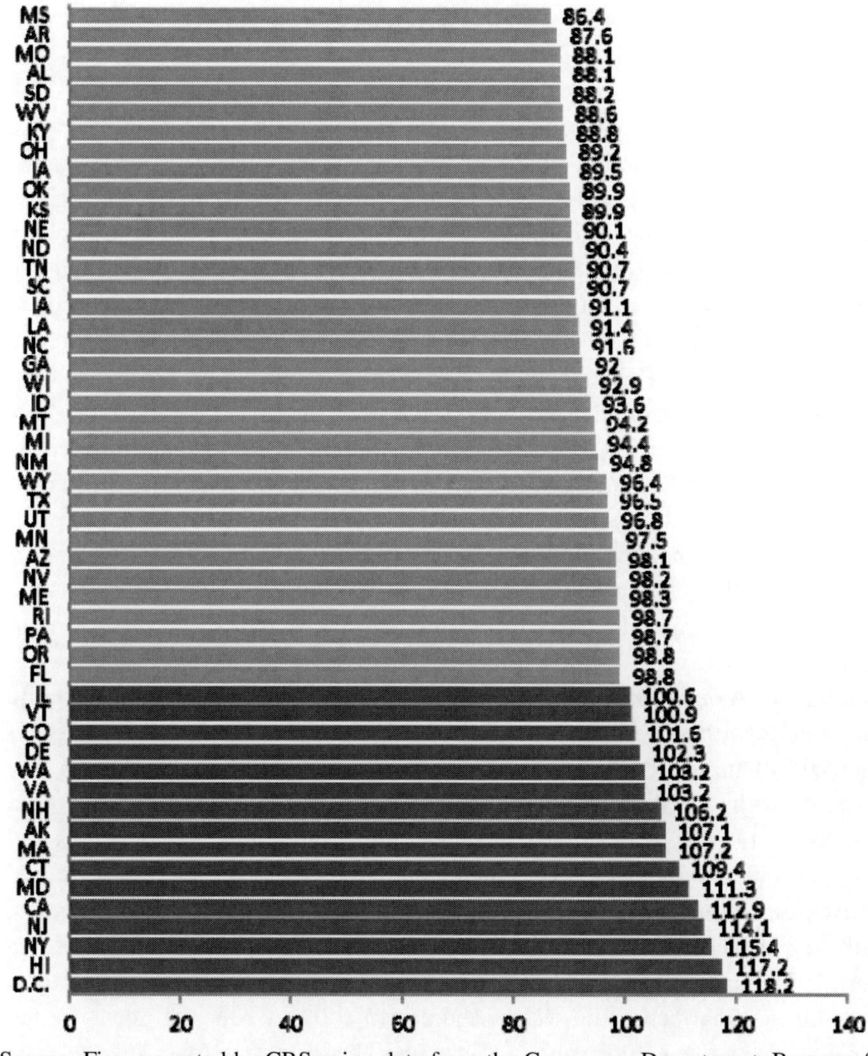

Source: Figure created by CRS using data from the Commerce Department, Bureau of Economic Analysis, "Real Personal Income for States and Metropolitan Areas, 2008-2012," press release, April 24, 2014, https://www.bea.gov/newsreleases /regional/rpp/rpp_newsrelease.htm.

Note: Dark-shaded bars indicate an index greater than 100.

Figure 12. BEA Regional Price Parities by State, 2012.

GINI INDEX

The Gini index is a popular summary measure of income dispersion that describes the relationship between the cumulative distribution of income and the cumulative distribution of the population, a relationship depicted by the Lorenz curve.[36] It is used to assess changes in income dispersion for a given population over time and make comparisons across groups, especially international comparisons. The Lorenz curve (**Figure 13**) plots the cumulative percentage of the population in ascending order of income (i.e., from poor to rich) on the horizontal axis against the cumulative percentage of total income on the vertical axis. Points along the Lorenz curve indicate the portion of total income held by a particular segment of the population. The straight grey line in **Figure 13** shows what the Lorenz curve would look like if total income was equally distributed. Under that scenario, for example, 50% of total income would be held by the (poorest) 50% of the population (point A), 75% of total income would be held by the (poorest) 75% of the population (point B), and so forth. This line is alternately referred to as *the line of equality* or the equidistribution line. The curved line illustrates the Lorenz curve under a more realistic scenario, in which income is dispersed unevenly across the population. As more income is concentrated at the top of the distribution, the curve pulls farther away from the equidistribution line. The Gini coefficient is the ratio of the area between the Lorenz curve and the equidistribution line (area A) to the total area underneath the equidistribution line (area A + area B). As the Lorenz curve approaches the equidistribution line, area A falls and the Gini index value declines. Perfect equality occurs when the Lorenz curve overlaps the equidistribution line and there is no area between the two curves, reducing the Gini to zero. When a single household holds all income— the perfect inequality scenario—the Lorenz curve runs along the horizontal axis up until the final percentile where it jumps to 100%. Under this scenario, the area between the equidistribution line and the Lorenz curve and the area underneath the equidistribution line are the same (area A + area B), producing a Gini index value of one.

As demonstrated above, Gini index values range from zero to one, with zero indicating perfect equality (i.e., all individuals hold the same income) and one indicating perfect inequality (i.e., all income is held by one household). It provides a convenient way to compare the distribution of income over time or the income distributions for different groups, with higher values indicating greater dispersion. However, the index has drawbacks as well. For example, the Gini index does not convey information about the shape of the income distribution; several different shapes can yield the same Gini index value. **Figure 14** provides an example of two Lorenz curves that both produce a Gini value of 0.20. The Gini is also not perfectly decomposable, which means it is not well-suited for comparing the dispersion of income *within* groups to the dispersion *between* groups.

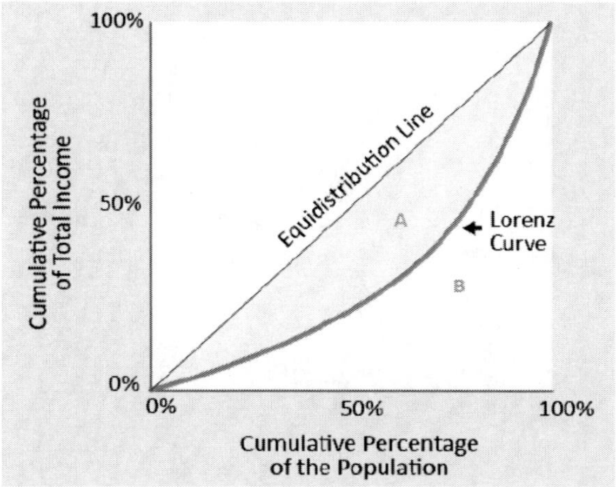

Source: CRS.

Figure 13. The Relationship Between the Lorenz Curve and Gini Index.

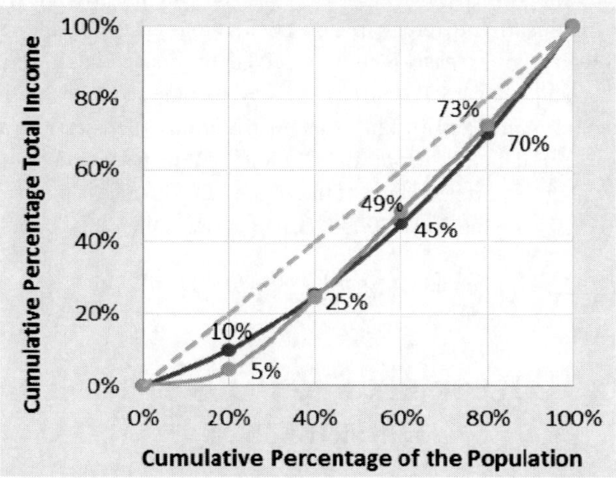

Source: Graph constructed by CRS based on an example provided in Lorenzo Giovanni Bellu and Paolo Liberati, *Inequality Analysis: the Gini Index*, Food and Agricultural Organization of the United Nations, EASYPOL Module 40, December 2006, http://www.fao.org/tc/easypol.

Notes: Both Lorenz curves yield a Gini index of 0.20

Figure 14. Two Lorenz Curves with the Same Gini Index.

Figure 15 plots the Gini index between 1993 and 2013 and shows an upward trend. Over this time period, the Gini index for the United States ranged from 0.450 (in 1995) to 0.477 (in 2011). It was 0.476 in 2013.

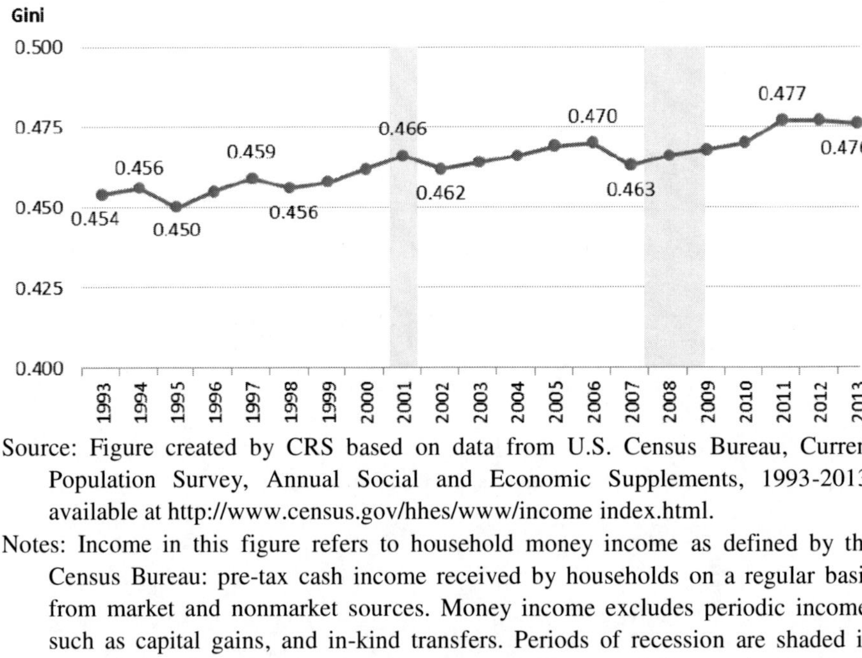

Source: Figure created by CRS based on data from U.S. Census Bureau, Current Population Survey, Annual Social and Economic Supplements, 1993-2013, available at http://www.census.gov/hhes/www/income index.html.

Notes: Income in this figure refers to household money income as defined by the Census Bureau: pre-tax cash income received by households on a regular basis from market and nonmarket sources. Money income excludes periodic income, such as capital gains, and in-kind transfers. Periods of recession are shaded in gray. Recession data are from the National Bureau of Economic Research, http://www.nber.org/cycles and reflect the 2001 recession (March 2001-November 2001) and the 2007-2009 recession (December 2007-June 2009).

Figure 15. Gini Index for the United States, 1993-2013.

APPENDIX A. DESCRIBING INCOMES AT THE TOP OF THE DISTRIBUTION

Survey data, like the CPS-ASEC used by the Census Bureau to describe the distribution of household money income cannot be used to identify with certainty the highest and lowest earners in the population (See "Census Data"). IRS data are superior for studying incomes at the top, but privacy rules limit the information the IRS can share publicly about filers, though it does provide some information. For example, IRS is required by law to report (in aggregate) on the number of filers with adjusted gross incomes above $200,000, and it produces occasional reports on the top 400 filers, considered in aggregate and with identifying information removed.[37]

Through data agreements with both agencies, the Congressional Budget Office (CBO) is able to combine CPS and IRS data to create a more comprehensive picture of the income distribution than could be obtained from either data set used alone. As part of their analysis, CBO describes the distribution of incomes within the top 20% of households.

Figure A-1 shows average after-tax income within the top quintile for 2011 as reported by CBO. CBO data indicate a wide range of incomes at the top of the income spectrum. The top 20% of households received $188,200 on average in after-tax income in 2011. Average income among the top 1% was $1,031,900. While mean income among the top 1% is high relative to the overall quintile mean, it is likely to lie far below incomes of the highest earners. For reference, IRS analysis of the top 400 filers in 2009 revealed that average adjusted-gross income among them was $202 million.[38]

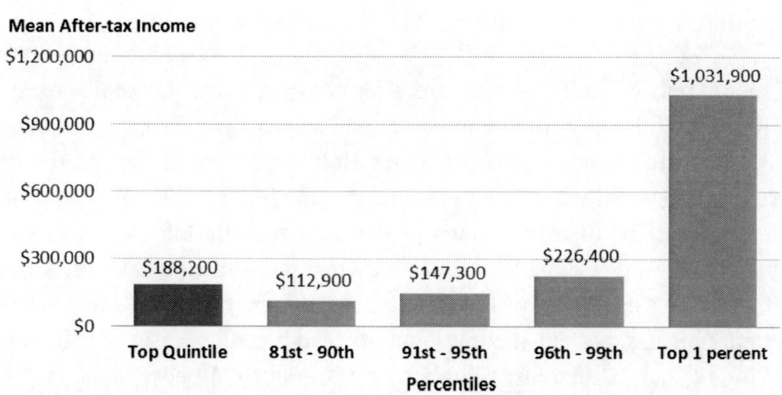

Source: Prepared by CRS using data from the Congressional Budget Office, *The Distribution of Household Income and Federal Taxes, 2011*, December 2014, Supplemental Data, available from https://www.cbo.gov/publication/ 49440.

Notes: Income in this figure refers to after-tax household income as defined by CBO: the sum of market income and government transfers, less federal tax liabilities. CBO defines market income as labor income, business income, capital gains realized from the sale of assets, capital income excluding capital gains, and income received in retirement for past services or from other sources. CBO defines government transfers as both cash and in-kind benefits.

Figure A-1. Mean After-Tax Income within the Top Income Quintile, 2011.

Appendix B. Summary Indicators Reported by Census

The U.S. Census Bureau publishes several summary measures of income dispersion in its annual *Income and Poverty in the United States* report: the Gini index, mean log deviation of income (MLD), Theil index, and Atkinson index. These indicators differ from the measures described in the main body of this report in that they do not convey descriptive details on the experience of the typical household, the range of incomes, or the shape of the distribution, but instead use information on the full distribution to characterize overall income dispersion (i.e., they are relative measures used to assess departure from a perfectly equal distribution of income). While the Gini is familiar to many (and discussed in this report—see "Gini Index"), the other three measures are less so. This appendix provides an overview of the MLD, Theil, and Atkinson indices, explaining their basic properties and interpretation, and the value they bring to analysis of the income distribution.

Generalized Entropy Indices: MLD and Theil Index

General entropy (GE) indices are a family of relative inequality measures that are based on ratios of incomes to the mean. A sensitivity parameter—typically identified using the Greek letter alpha—adjusts the weight the index gives to various portions of the distribution and distinguishes members of the broader class of GE measures. Two of the most popular GE measures are the MLD and Theil index, which are defined when the sensitivity parameter is set to zero and one, respectively. They are bounded from below by zero, the value that communicates perfect income equality. Both indices rise in value as the dispersion of income increases; higher values indicate a wider dispersion (i.e., more unequal distribution). Unlike the Gini, general entropy indices are not capped at one.

The MLD and Theil index share several attractive features. They are scale invariant, meaning that the value does not change when all incomes are multiplied by a constant. This is helpful because it means, for example, that the measure is not sensitive to currency conversion. They also respond in an intuitive way to transfers of income within a distribution. Namely, they will register more dispersion when income is transferred from households at the bottom to those at the top.[39] Finally, they are perfectly decomposable by subgroups. Both measures permit within and between components to be identified separately (e.g., they can be used to assess the extent to which a change in income dispersion is due to changes within U.S. states and how much can be explained by changes between states).

The MLD and Theil differ, however, in their sensitivity to changes at various parts of the income distribution. MLD is sensitive to changes at the bottom of the distribution, and will be more responsive than the Theil index to increased dispersion among low to middle incomes. The Theil index, on the other hand, will rise faster than the MLD as incomes at the top of the distribution grow disproportionately.[40] As such, it is possible to compare changes in income dispersion across portions of the distribution (lower tail, middle, or upper tail) by observing how the MLD and Theil index change over time for a given income distribution.

The Atkinson Index

The Atkinson index is a welfare-based measure. It uses a specific mathematical function to quantify the "social welfare" of a given income distribution and compares it to the value the same social welfare function would have if total income was distributed with perfect mathematical equality. The interpretation given to the numerical value of the index is the proportion of total income a society would be willing to forfeit to achieve a perfectly equal distribution. For example, consider a society with 100 individuals and a total (societal) income of $1 million. An Atkinson index of 0.10 indicates that this society would be equally content with 90% of total income (i.e., $900,000) *if it were distributed equally* among all 100 members (i.e., all members earn $9,000), as they are with the actual distribution of (actual) total income. The Atkinson index values range from 0 to 1, with 0 indicating that total income is distributed with perfectly mathematical equality (i.e., society would be willing to give up none of its total income to achieve an equal distribution, because they are already there).

Like general entropy indices, the Atkinson index is a parameterized measure. The Atkinson sensitivity parameter—denoted by the Greek letter epsilon and often called the *inequality aversion parameter*—varies the priority applied to incomes at the lower end of the distribution in the social welfare function. As epsilon increases, so does the weight given to lower-income households and the value of the Atkinson index for a given income distribution.

Like the MLD and Theil index, the Atkinson index is scale invariant, meaning that the index value does not change when all incomes are multiplied by a constant. It also registers more inequality, for a given inequality aversion parameter, as income is transferred from the bottom to the top of the income distribution. Unlike the MLD and Theil index, however, the Atkinson index is not easily decomposable into within and between components.[41]

End Notes

[1] For a related discussion of U.S. income distribution trends, see CRS Report RS20811, *The Distribution of Household Income and the Middle Class*, by Craig K. Elwell.

[2] This report focuses on income. It does not address the measurement and distribution of wealth. Although income and wealth concepts are closely related, they are not the same. Income refers to a *flow* of resources, some of which are consumed in the present period and the remainder (if any) added to the *stock* of resources, i.e., wealth.

[3] Studies that compare income definitions and levels of aggregation find that definitional differences matter to income levels, distribution, and the tracking of income trends. For example, see Congressional Budget Office, *The Distribution of Household Income and Federal Taxes, 2010*, December 2013, http://www.cbo.gov/publication/44604; and Richard V. Burkhauser, Jeff Larrimore, and Kosali Simon, *A "Second Opinion" on the Economic Health of the American Middle Class*, National Bureau of Economic Research, Working Paper 17164, June 2011, http://www.nber.org/papers/ w17164.

[4] There is also some debate over whether income or monetized consumption is the more appropriate measure of living standards. Consumption may more accurately reflect purchasing power, including a household's ability to provide for basic needs. Looking at income alone can mask the economic effects of uncertainty (e.g., risk of job loss), capital loss (e.g., foreclosure), and large differences in prices. These events affect day-to-day economic security and can result in reduced consumption even while income remains steady. In contrast, a drop in income does not necessarily translate into consumption loss if households spend out of their savings or prices fall, or if the measure of income does not include transfer payments (e.g., social programs) or other, informal forms of insurance (e.g., family support networks).

[5] The Current Population Survey (CPS) Table Creator allows users to view a range of statistics using its pre-defined alternative income measures and construct their own income measures by selecting from among 42 Census-defined income components. The CPS Table Creator is available online from http://www.census.gov/cps/data/ cpstablecreator.html.

[6] Capital gains and losses are included conceptually by Census in their definitions for disposable income and market income, but Census no longer produces estimates of capital gains and losses. The last year for which capital gains and losses estimates are available from the CPS Table Creator is 2007 (data collected in 2008). The decision to halt production of these estimates was influenced by the two-year delay in access to IRS's individual income tax records (the primary data source for capital gains and losses estimates).

[7] The Survey of Consumer Finance (SCF, see footnote 14) data show that households in the top income group are more likely to hold public stock (a capital gains earning asset) and have higher mean stockholding values than households at the bottom of the distribution. In 2013,

the stock ownership rate among families in the lower 20% of the income distribution was 4.2%, whereas it was 45.4% for families in the top 10% of the income distribution. Preliminary SCF numbers reveal that, among families that held stock, the mean value of stockholdings for families in the bottom 20% of the income distribution was $55,500 in 2013, whereas it was $694,200 among families in the top 10%. Board of Governors of the Federal Reserve System, "2013 Survey of Consumer Finances, Historic Tables and Charts Based on Internal Data," September 4, 2014, http://www.federalreserve.gov/econresdata /scf/scfindex.htm.

[8] See, for example, Philip Armour, Richard V. Burkhauser, and Jeff Larrimore, "Levels and Trends in U.S. Income and its Distribution: A Crosswalk from Market Income towards a Comprehensive Haig-Simons Income Approach," *Southern Economic Journal*, vol. 81, no. 2 (2014), pp. 271-293.

[9] A discussion of both viewpoints is provided by Thomas B. Edsall, "What if We're Looking at Inequality the Wrong Way?," *The New York Times*, June 26, 2013, http://opinionator.blogs.

[10] The Congressional Budget Office (CBO) compared the 2011 U.S. income distribution before and after accounting for taxes, finding a "slightly more" compressed distribution when tax deductions and credits are applied. CBO, *The Distribution of Household Income and Federal Taxes, 2011*, November 2014, https://www.cbo.gov/publication/49440.

[11] Census produces annual estimates of the fungible value of Medicaid or Medicare, but does not include these estimates in any of their pre-defined income measures. Instead, they permit data users to include Medicare and/or Medicaid estimates when customizing income measures. This value is calculated based on the extent to which the programs free up resources that otherwise could have been used to purchase medical care or insurance. Robert W. Cleveland, *Alternative Income Estimates in the United States: 2003*, U.S. Census Bureau, P60-288, June 2005, https://www.census.gov/hhes/www/income/publications/cps-reports.html. CBO accounts for health insurance programs, including Medicare, Medicare, and CHIP in its analyses of the U.S. income distribution, using the average cost to the government of providing the benefit. CBO departed from the Census methods of estimating government-provided health insurance in 2012 with its analysis of the 2008 and 2009 U.S. income distributions. Details on CBO's treatment of health care benefits are reported in CBO, *The Distribution of Household Income and Federal Taxes, 2008 and 2009*, July 2012, http://www.cbo.ogv/publication/43373.

[12] The Census Bureau, for example, provides equivalence-adjusted estimates for some but not all of its income dispersion estimates to account for differences in membership numbers and composition (i.e., that children consume less on average than adults, and the impacts of economies of scale that derive from the sharing of resources and expenses within families). See Carmen DeNavas-Walt and Bernadette D. Proctor, *Income and Poverty in the United States: 2013*, U.S. Census Bureau, Current Population Reports P60-249, September 2014, http://www.census.gov/. The CBO also adjusts household income for membership, treating adults and children equally. See CBO, *The Distribution of Household Income and Federal Taxes, 2011*, November 2014, https://www.cbo.gov/publication/49440.

[13] The Panel Survey of Income Dynamics (PSID), which is run by the University of Michigan, is a popular (and nongovernment) source of data on incomes in the United States. For more information on the PSID, see http://psidonline.isr.umich.edu/.

[14] The SCF is another source of data on income in the United States. The SCF is a cross-sectional survey administered every three years under the auspices of the Federal Reserve Board to collect information on the assets and liabilities (among other characteristics) of U.S. households. Although the SCF collects income data, its main strength is the span and detail

of information collected on household wealth. Additional information is available at http://www.federalreserve.gov/econresdata/scf/aboutscf.htm.

[15] CBO uses both Census and IRS data in its analysis of the distribution of household income and federal taxes. CBO does not provide public access to its household-level data, but rich supplemental data tables on the CBO website provide useful details and complement the analysis provided in its reports. Because of delayed access to IRS data, the CBO analysis applies to a past-year(s) income distribution. The most recent report describes the 2011 income distribution. For more information, see CBO, *The Distribution of Household Income and Federal Taxes, 2011*, December 2014, Supplemental Data, available at https://www.cbo.gov/publication/49440.

[16] The ASEC is also referred to as the *March Supplement* because it is administered largely in March of each year.

[17] Older versions of this report also looked at health insurance coverage. The Census Bureau began reporting separately on health insurance in 2014. For Census statistics on income and poverty for 2013, see Carmen DeNavas-Walt and Bernadette D. Proctor, *Income and Poverty in the United States: 2013*, U.S. Census Bureau, Current Population Reports P60-249, September 2014, http://www.census.gov/.

[18] Variable censoring at the point of data capture and processing for the CPS-ASEC sample is likely to be rare. Based on data collected in the 2000 survey, Welniak reports that no households in the sample reported earnings income above the data-capture limit and only 26 households reported earnings income above the processing limit. See Edward J. Welniak, *Measuring Household Income Inequality Using the CPS*, Internal Revenue Service, Statistics of Income Division, Special Studies in Federal Tax Statistics, 2003, pp. 3-13.

[19] The CPS-ASEC records information for dozens of income categories for each individual aged 15 or older, for up to 16 persons per household. It collects data on four categories of earned-income: (1) wage and salary income from longest job-held, (2) other wage and salary income, (3) nonfarm self-employment income, and (4) farm self-employment income.

[20] Additional data editing is applied to public-release data to preserve confidentiality of the CPS-ASEC survey respondents. Historically, income data were censored above a Census-determined maximum value. This maximum value changed from year to year, and it was typically selected to be the 97th percentile of income (for a particular income source). Incomes greater than the maximum value were either replaced by the maximum value (prior to 1996) or the mean of values above the maximum (1996-2010). Starting in 2011, Census employed a new method to provide confidentiality protections called rank proximity swapping. Using this method, (edited) income values are swapped between individuals with similar income ranks for all individuals in the top 3% of income. For more information, see Carmen DeNavas-Walt and Bernadette D. Proctor, *Income and Poverty in the United States: 2013*, U.S. Census Bureau, Current Population Reports P60-249, September 2014, p. 61.

[21] The 2014 version of the CPS-ASEC was redesigned with this limitation in mind, and it attempts to measure interest, dividend, and pension income more accurately.

[22] The SCF (see footnote 14) also provides information on incomes and assets at the top of the distribution.

[23] For more information, see CRS Report R40411, *The Economic Effects of Capital Gains Taxation*, by Thomas L. Hungerford.

[24] Charles F. Manski, "Income Tax and Labor Supply: Let's Acknowledge What We Don't Know," *VOX (CEPR)*, August 23, 2012, http://www.voxeu.org/article/income

[25] Most data are from Carmen DeNavas-Walt and Bernadette D. Proctor, *Income and Poverty in the United States: 2013*, U.S. Census Bureau, Current Population Reports P60-249, September 2014. Additional Census data are taken from supplemental tables, available at http://www.census.gov/hhes/www/income

[26] The most recent year of data available is 2013.

[27] For more information, see http://www.bls.gov/cpi/cpirsdc.htm.

[28] This is not to say that the mean is without value. Among other uses, the mean provides a meaningful indicator of total group income, adjusted for population size. It can be used to compare resources across groups when distribution within groups is not of primary interest.

[29] Because income by some definitions can be negative, the range is not necessarily equivalent to the income of the top earner (i.e., as it would if the bottom income by definition was zero).

[30] Money income can take on negative values because it includes income from business sources (such as commercial farms), which can record losses.

[31] Likewise, a left-skewed distribution will have a mean-to-median ratio that is less than one.

[32] Mean and median household incomes were $65,766 and $49,594 (in 2013 CPI-U-RS adjusted dollars), respectively, in 1993. In 2013, mean household income was $72,641 and median household income was $51,939.

[33] A rise in the mean-to-median ratio does not necessarily imply growth at the top, since growth in income below the median can push up the mean as well. If income among low-income households rises disproportionately and median income growth does not match pace, the ratio can rise without an accompanying rise in the spread of data.

[34] Two important notes are in order. First, this does not mean that all households within a given quintile experienced income growth. Some households' incomes grew at rates above their quintile average, some grew at rates below their quintile average, and some experienced income loss. Second, households do not necessarily stay in a given quintile from year to year. So, for example, the households that comprise the middle quintile in 2013 may not be the households that comprise the middle quintile in 2003 or 1993. Analysis of microdata is needed to examine income dynamics.

[35] To be clear, the percentage points shown in **Figure 9** are a *relative* measure that describe quintile shares of total income (i.e., how "the pie" is divided across household income groups). But the *change* in percentage point is measured in absolute terms, not as a percentage of its base value.

[36] Mathematically, the Gini coefficient is based on the average absolute difference between all random pairs of incomes normalized by the mean.

[37] The Tax Act of 1976 (P.L. 94-455) requires the IRS to publish information on individual tax returns for $200,000 or more; for more information, see http://www.irs.gov/uac/SOI

[38] See http://www.irs.gov/uac/SOI-

[39] This is known as the *principle of transfer*, one of several measures used to assess income dispersion measures.

[40] More generally, when the sensitivity parameter is small and positive, the index is more responsive to changes at the bottom of the distribution. As it takes higher, positive values, the index is more sensitive to changes at the top of the distribution.

[41] The Atkinson index can be transformed into a generalized entropy measure that is perfectly decomposable into within and between components. The formula for this transformation and additional information is in Lorenzo Giovanni Bellu and Paolo Liberati, *Policy Impacts on Inequality: Welfare-based Measures of Inequality, The Atkinson Index*, Food and Agriculture Organization of the United Nations, EASYPol Module 50, December 2006.

In: Income Distribution in the United States ISBN: 978-1-63482-675-4
Editor: Clayton Diaz

Chapter 2

THE DISTRIBUTION OF HOUSEHOLD INCOME AND THE MIDDLE CLASS*

Craig K. Elwell

SUMMARY

Although not itself a subject of legislation, the shape of the income distribution enters Congress's decision-making process concerning such policy issues as taxes, means-tested benefits, and social insurance programs. Congress also considers legislation specifically in the name of those in the middle class, which is variously defined as some income level or income range within the distribution of U.S. households with income. After briefly analyzing the distribution of household money income in 2012, the report attempts to put the term "middle class" into greater perspective.

The first key point of the report is that, although there are a variety of ways to describe the income distribution, all show that income is concentrated among high-income households. Of the 122,459,000 households with income in 2012, 2.3% had incomes of at least $250,000. (The Census Bureau does not disaggregate income within the $250,000-or-more income class.) In addition, a large share of total money income accrues to those at the upper end of the distribution. In 2012, the top 5%

* This is an edited, reformatted and augmented version of a Congressional Research Service publication RS20811, prepared for Members and Committees of Congress dated March 10, 2014.

of U.S. households with income accounted for 22.3% of total income, and the top 20% of households (which includes the top 5%) had 51.0% of all money income. A broader definition of household income, incorporating capital gains, the value of non-cash benefits (e.g., Food Stamps, Medicare and Medicaid, and employer paid health insurance), and subtracting estimates of federal taxes, tends to make the income distribution slightly more equal.

The second major point is that there is no official government definition of who belongs to the middle class, and the term means different things to different people. The middle class may refer to a group with a common point of view or to those having similar incomes, for example.

Third, absolute income appears to partly determine who belongs to the middle class. By combining money income data from the latest Annual Social and Economic Supplement to the Current Population Survey with results from surveys that asked people to identify their social class, the middle class may refer to households with income levels in 2012 that ranged from $39,736 (the bottom of the middle quintile, 20%, of households) and extended into the top quintile (households with income of $104,087 or more)—perhaps including households with incomes somewhat over $200,000.

Last, relative income may also be a defining characteristic of the middle class. In other words, the middle class appears to identify itself relative to the income of a reference group (e.g., their neighbors or coworkers). According to studies of self-reported well-being, those who constitute the middle class seemingly are of like minds with regard to their economic situation. Specifically, having incomes far above those at the lower end of the income distribution generally correlates with satisfaction to the middle class, but when those at the upper end of the distribution fare much better than they do, the level of middle-class satisfaction is generally lessened.

The shape of the income distribution is not itself a subject of legislation, but Members of Congress appear to consider it in their decision-making process concerning a number of policy issues such as taxes, means-tested benefits, and social insurance programs. Congress also takes up legislation specifically in the name of those in the middle (however defined) of the income distribution who commonly are referred to as the middle class. Some Members have, for example, proposed bills to improve U.S. competitiveness as a means of increasing exports manufactured by workers in "good" (middle-class) jobs. (For example, P.L. 111-240, the Small Business Jobs Act of 2010.) Similarly, training policy generally has been crafted to provide individuals with the skills thought necessary to attain a middle-class standard of living. (For example, P.L. 105-220, the Authorization of the Workforce Investment Act.)

This report first presents a brief analysis of the distribution of income across households in 2012, the latest year for which annual data are available from the Census Bureau.[1] It then attempts to put the term middle class into greater perspective: first, by applying results from public opinion surveys on social class to the Census Bureau's data on the income distribution in 2012; and second, by reviewing findings from empirical studies on the contribution of relative (as opposed to absolute) income to the identity of the middle class.

THE DISTRIBUTION OF HOUSEHOLD INCOME

The Census Bureau conducts a survey from which it derives annual estimates of the distribution of income across households, families, and individuals with income.[2] Households, which are more numerous than families, appear to be most relevant to the discussion here because household members are assumed to pool whatever income they have and share a common standard of living.[3]

The bureau's official measure of income is "money income." It includes earnings, interest, dividends, pensions, child support, and government non means-tested income (e.g., Social Security benefits, unemployment compensation, and veterans' payments). Money income is calculated on a pre-tax basis; that is, it excludes payments for personal income taxes, Social Security, Medicare, union dues, etc. It also excludes the value of non-cash means-tested benefits (e.g., food stamps, public housing subsidies), employer-provided fringe benefits, and capital gains. Money income is the measure on which official estimates of poverty are based.[4]

Data describing the distribution of income across households can be presented in a number of ways. The top portion of *Table 1* displays the number and share of households with income by income class. The income class sizes range from about $5,000 toward the lower end of the distribution to about $50,000 at the upper end of the distribution. In 2012, 2.1% of households (2,549,000 out of 122,459,000) had incomes between $200,000 and $249,999, for example. Another 2.4% of households (2,911,000 out of 122,459,000) had incomes of $250,000 or more. (The Census Bureau does not disaggregate income within the group of households with incomes of $250,000 or more.) At the lower end of the distribution, 3.4% of households (4,204,000 out of 122,459,000) had incomes of less than $5,000.

Table 1. Distribution of Household Money Income by Selected Income Class, 2012

Income Class	# of Households (in thousands)		% of Households
All Households	122,459		100.0
Less than $5,000	4,204		3.4
$5,000 to $9,999	4,729		3.9
$10,000 to $14,999	6,982		5.7
$15,000 to $19,999	7,157		5.8
$20,000 to $24,999	7,131		5.5
$25,000 to $29,999	6,740		5.4
$30,000 to $34,999	6,354		5.2
$35,000 to $39,999	5,832		4.8
$40,000 to $44,999	5,547		4.5
$45,000 to $49,999	5,254		4.4
$50,000 to $59,999	9,358		7.6
$60,000 to $69,999	8,305		6.8
$70,000 to $79,999	7,170		5.9
$80,000 to $89,999	5,969		4.9
$90,000 to $99,999	4,901		4.0
$100,000 to $124,999	9,490		7.7
$125,000 to $149,999	5,759		4.7
$150,000 to $199,999	6,116		5.0
$200,000 to $249,999	2,549		2.1
$250,000 and above	2,911		2.4
Median Income		$51.017	
Mean Income		$71,274	

Source: U.S. Census Bureau, 2012 Annual Social and Economic Supplement to the Current Population Survey.

The concentration of income among the relatively few households in the upper tail of the income distribution can be seen by comparing two summary measures of the shape of the income distribution shown in the last two rows of *Table 1*. One summary measure, median income, is the level below and above which one-half of all households lie. It is generally considered a better indication of the income of the “typical” household than is the mean (average), which can be pulled up by a relatively small number of high income households in the upper end of the distribution. One-half of households had income above the median of $51,017 in 2012, whereas many fewer households (about one-third) had income above the mean of $71,274.

Another often-used way to describe the distribution of income is the share of total money income going to different household groups in order of increasing income. In 2012, there were a total of 122,459,000 households with income, so each quintile (fifth) in the distribution represents 24,492,000 households. The Census Bureau separately calculates the total income share of the top 5% of households. As shown in *Table 2*, the top 5% of households accounted for 22.3% of all income in 2012. By comparison, the lowest quintile (20%) of households had only 3.2% of aggregate income.

Table 2. Census Bureau Estimate: Distribution of Household Money Income by Quintile, 2012

	Quintiles					
	Lowest	Second	Third	Fourth	Highest	Top 5%
Number of households	24,492,000	24,492,000	24,492,000	24,492,000	24,492,000	6,126,000
Range of income class	$20,592	$20,593	$39,736	$64,554	$104,087	$191,150
	or less	to $39,735	to $64,553	to $104,086	or more	or more
Share of household income (%)	3.2	8.3	14.4	23.0	51.0	22.3

Source: U.S. Census Bureau, 2012 Annual Social and Economic Supplement to the Current Population Survey.

The Congressional Budget Office (CBO) produces annual estimates of the U.S. income distribution that combines information from the CPS with Statistics of Income (SOI) compiled by the Internal Revenue Service. This richer data set allows CBO to construct a broader definition of household income than found in the Census's money income estimates. Major sources of difference in CBO's estimate of household income are the inclusion of capital gains and the value of non-cash benefits (such as Food Stamps, Medicare and Medicaid, and employer paid health insurance premiums). The use of the SOI also allows CBO to compute after-tax income by subtracting estimates of federal income and corporate taxes, social insurance (payroll) taxes, and excise taxes from before-tax income. Because SOI data are not as timely as Census data and because of the computational scope of the task, the most recent CBO income distribution estimate is for 2010 (released in December 2013).[5]

As shown in *Table 3*, CBO's estimate of the 2010 distribution of household income is broadly similar to the Census estimate. However, because of transfers and taxes, CBO's estimate of the income distribution is modestly more equal than the Census estimate (for 2012). CBO's broader treatment of transfers increases the share of income in the lowest quintile. In addition, CBO's consideration of the federal tax system decreases (relative to CBO's estimate of the before-tax share) the after-tax share of the highest quintile and increases the share of the four lower quintiles.

Table 3. CBO Estimate: Distribution of Before and After-Tax Household Income by Quintile, 2010

	Quintiles					
	Lowest	Second	Third	Fourth	Highest	Top 5%
Share of before-tax household income (%)	5.1	9.6	14.2	20.4	51.9	27.4
Share of after-tax household income (%)	6.2	10.9	15.4	21.0	48.1	24.3

Source: Congressional Budget Office, Distribution of Household Income and Federal Taxes, December 2013.

THE MIDDLE CLASS

Although Congress often considers legislation specifically in the name of the middle class, there is no official government definition of the group, and it is not the aim of this report to develop one. What constitutes the middle class is subjective and comparative, meaning different things to different people. The term may refer to a group with a common point of view or to those having similar incomes. Most people likely have decided views as to whether they are middle class, and those who refer to the middle class have a rough idea of whom they have in mind. How closely these definitions correspond is another matter.

Absolute Income

Any discussion of the middle class necessarily starts with those at the very middle of the income distribution. As previously discussed, median household income was $51,017 in 2012. How far the middle class stretches above and below the median is the question.

A narrow view of the middle class might include only those in the middle (third) quintile, that is, those households with money income between $39,736 and $64,553 in 2012 (see *Table 2*). It seems unlikely, however, that so narrow an income range would account completely for those commonly considered to be middle class. For that reason, the three middle quintiles are often combined to broaden the definition. In 2012, according to this broader definition, the 73,476,000 households with income above $20,592 and below $104,087 might have composed the middle class. These 60% of all households in the distribution accounted for a smaller share (45.7%) of total income in 2012.

A still broader definition of middle class can be constructed by adding that part of the top quintile up to the point at which the top 5% of households begins. In 2012, then, 91,842,000 households with incomes above $20,592 and below $191,150 might have composed the middle class. These 75% of all households in the distribution accounted for a slightly smaller share (74.4%) of total household income in that year.

The results of opinion surveys offer further insight into the income bounds that may define the middle class. A few surveys asked people to indicate their social class. In a 2005 *New York Times* survey, for example, 35% of respondents identified themselves as working class and 7% said they were part of the lower class. Another 42% considered themselves to be middle class and 15% said they were part of the upper middle class, whereas 1% of respondents identified themselves as members of the upper class.[6] In contrast, the top income class ($250,000 or more) in the Census Bureau's detailed data on the household income distribution shown in *Table 1* accounted for 2.3% of all households. Assuming some correspondence between the survey responses and Census income data, this discrepancy suggests that the 15% of respondents who said they were upper-middle class includes some households with incomes over $250,000. Comparing just the 42% of respondents who reported being middle class with the Census data suggests that the upper bound of the middle class might instead be lower at somewhat under $125,000. The lower bound of the middle class might be just over $40,000, based on a comparison of the 42% of respondents who reported they were working or lower class with the Census data.

The National Opinion Research Center (NORC) at the University of Chicago began asking people in 1972 to identify their social class in the General Social Survey (GSS). The cumulative results of self-reported class divisions in the GSS can be compared with the Census income distribution as was done above with the *Times* survey. According to the 1972-2010 GSS data,[7] 3.2% of the population consider themselves to be upper class. This would put the dividing line between middle and upper class at somewhat over $200,000. The 1972-2010 GSS results further indicate that 5.7% of the population consider themselves to be lower class and 45.7% identified themselves as working class. This would put the lower income level for the middle class at just over $50,000.

As part of a larger study of the middle class, the Pew Research Center sampled opinions regarding social class in 2012. It found that 51% of surveyed adults living in households with incomes between $30,000 and $49,999 identified themselves as middle class and 65% of surveyed adults with household incomes between $50,000 and $99,999 identified themselves as middle class. Although these results suggest that the income boundaries of the middle class might extend from $30,000 to $99,999, the finding that 46% of surveyed adults with household incomes of $100,000 or more self-identified as middle class suggests that the upper bound of the middle class might exceed $100,000. But by how much? The Pew survey also found that 7% of Americans consider themselves to be lower class; 25%, lower middle class; 49%, middle class; 15%, upper middle class; and 2%, upper class.[8] If the 15% of survey respondents who considered themselves upper middle class were added to the middle class rather than upper class category as Pew has done, then the upper bound of the middle class might be somewhat over $200,000.

Taken together, the survey responses suggest that the lower bound of the middle class might start in the middle (third) quintile of the income distribution shown in *Table 2* (households with income of $39,736 to $64,553). The surveys' results further suggest that the middle class extends into the top (fifth) quintile of the income distribution (households with income of $104,087 or more)—perhaps including households with income somewhat over $200,000.[9]

Relative Income

The satisfaction (utility) that households derive from their income appears to be associated both with their absolute level of income and how that income level compares with the incomes of others.[10] While the middle class may be content with absolute income levels that afford them a much better-than-subsistence standard of living, the satisfaction of the middle class also may be affected by their income relative to a reference group. If individuals care about how their income compares with that of their neighbors or coworkers, for example, it lends support to the notion of like-income groups possessing a shared outlook on economic (and perhaps other) policy.

Since the 1990s, economists have increasingly turned their attention to identifying factors that contribute to utility (well-being or happiness), including one's position relative to others.[11] One study, for example, analyzed whether group-specific suicide rates are associated with interpersonal comparisons of income.[12] Daly and Wilson used the suicide rate as an indicator of current and expected future happiness, and developed three measures of relative income: the ratio of income at the 90th percentile to median income (90/50), the ratio of median income to income at the 10th percentile (50/10), and the ratio of income at the 90th percentile to income at the 10th percentile (90/10). Among their findings was that an increase in the 50/10 ratio was associated with a decrease in the suicide rate, and that an increase in the 90/50 ratio was associated with an increase in the suicide rate. That is to say, those in the middle-income group (the 50th percentile) were (a) happier the larger the gap was between them and those at the low end of the distribution and (b) unhappier the larger the gap was between them and those at the high end of the distribution. Daly and Wilson considered the results evidence that relative income influences a group's sense of well-being. More specifically, increases in inequality at the upper and lower tails of the income distribution appear to have opposite effects on the satisfaction of the middle-income group.

Luttmer also presented evidence that relative income is an important determinant of well-being.[13] He matched survey data on self-reported happiness and other measures of well-being (e.g., frequency of marital disagreements, score on a depression index) with income data by locality. Luttmer estimated that an increase in neighbors' income had a negative effect on one's own happiness. Dynan and Ravina built on Luttmer's study by using the GSS to assess the effect of differences in relative incomes over recent decades on happiness. Like Luttmer, they found that relative income is strongly associated with self-reported happiness. Dynan and Ravina further estimated that relative income most affects well-being when a group's income is above the average in its state but not at the top (90th percentile) of the income distribution. Or, as the authors put it, "relative concerns primarily affect people who have above-average income but are not extremely rich."[14]

Guven and Sorensen concluded that relative income plays a substantial role in explaining self-reported happiness among the middle-income group.[15] Because the GSS asks respondents how they think their income compares with that of the average family, the economists also were able to measure the relationship between happiness and perceived (as opposed to actual) relative income. Guven and Sorensen estimated that well-being is more affected by the perception of relative income than by actual relative income for the middle-income group. They further found that perceptions about relative income are more important in explaining the well-being of the middle-income group than the happiness of the low- and high-income groups.

The conclusions of these studies might not seem robust because they are based on self-assessments of well-being, but if they are correct, they appear relevant to the notion of like-minded income groups. Together, the studies suggest that the satisfaction of the middle class (however defined) depends not only on "keeping up with the Joneses" but also staying ahead of the Smiths, as Daly and Wilson put it in their study. In other words, whatever else they may have in common; those who may constitute the middle class seemingly have similar sentiments with regard to their economic situation. Specifically, having incomes far above those at the lower end of the income distribution generally correlates with satisfaction to the middle class, but when those at the upper end of the distribution fare much better than they do, the level of middle class satisfaction is generally lessened.

End Notes

[1] For information on trends in the distribution of income, see CRS Report R42400, The U.S. Income Distribution and Mobility: Trends and International Comparisons, by Linda Levine.

[2] The complete Census Bureau report (Income, Poverty, and Health Insurance: Coverage in the United States: 2012) is available at http://www.census.gov/prod/2013pubs/p60-245.pdf.

[3] In the Current Population Survey (CPS), a household is defined as all of the individuals who occupy a housing unit as their usual place of residence. A family is defined as a group of two or more individuals who reside together and who are related by birth, marriage, or adoption. A household may be composed of one or more families or no families at all; that is, a person living alone in a housing unit is counted in the CPS as a household.

[4] The Census Bureau periodically calculates alternative measures of income which can be used to assess the effects of federal (cash and noncash) transfers, capital gains, employee health benefits, return on own-home equity, federal and state income taxes, payroll taxes, and the Earned Income Tax Credit on the shape of the income distribution and on the number of persons living below the poverty threshold. The latest estimates cover 2009, and are available at http://www.census.gov/hhes/www/cpstables/032010/rdcall/toc.htm.

[5] CBO, "The Distribution of Household Income and Federal Taxes, 2010," December 2013, available at http://www.cbo.gov/sites/default/files/cbofiles/attachments/44604-AverageTaxRates.pdf.

[6] The New York Times published a series of articles in May 2005 under the title "Class Matters," which is available at http://www.nytimes.com/indexes/2005/05/15/ national/class/index.html.

[7] NORC, General Social Survey, http://www.norc.uchicago.edu/GSS+Website/.

[8] Pew Research Center, The Lost Decade of the Middle Class, August 22, 2012, available at http://www.pewsocialtrends.org/files/2012/08/pew-social-trends-lost-decade-of-the-middle-class.pdf. The results from the 2012 survey are similar to those from a 2008 survey conducted by Pew, Inside the Middle Class: Bad Times Hit the Good Life, available at http://pewsocialtrends.org/pubs/706/middle-class-poll.

[9] If those who consider themselves to be upper class were underrepresented in the surveys, the number of those who consider themselves to be upper class would be larger. If that is the case, the actual level of income that divides the middle from the upper class would be lower than is suggested by the surveys.

[10] Disagreement in the economics literature exists about the extent to which absolute versus relative income contributes to well-being and about what is the most appropriate measure of well-being. See, for example, Richard Ball and Kateryna Chernova, "Absolute Income, Relative Income, and Happiness," Social Indicators Research, September 2008, pp. 497-529; Daniel Kahneman and Angus Deaton, "High Income Improves Evaluation of Life but Not Emotional Well-Being," Proceedings of the National Academy of Sciences, vol. 107, no 38, September 2010, pp. 16489-16493; Richard Layard, Guy Mayraz and Stephen Nickell, Does Relative Income Matter? Are the Critics Right?, CEP Discussion Paper No. 918, March 2009; and Betsey Stevenson and Justin Wolfers, "Economic Growth and Subjective Well-Being: Reassessing the Easterlin Paradox," Brookings Papers on Economic Activity, 2008, pp. 1- 87.

[11] Andrew E. Clark, Paul Frijters, and Michael A. Shields, "Relative Income, Happiness, and Utility: An Explanation for the Easterlin Paradox and Other Puzzles," Journal of Economic Literature, vol. 46, no. 1 (2008), pp. 95-144.

[12] Mary Daly and Dan Wilson, "Keeping Up with the Joneses and Staying Ahead of the Smiths: Evidence from Suicide Data," Federal Reserve Bank of San Francisco Working Paper 2006-12, April 2006; and, Mary Daly, Dan Wilson, and Norman Johnson, "Relative Status and Well-Being: Evidence From U.S. Suicide Deaths," Federal Reserve Bank of San Francisco Working Paper 2012-16, September 2012, available at http://www.frbsf.org/economic-research/files/wp12- 16bk.pdf.

[13] Erzo F.P. Luttmer, "Neighbors as Negatives: Relative Earnings and Well-Being," Quarterly Journal of Economics, August 2005.

[14] Karen E. Dynan and Enrichetta Ravina, "Increasing Income Inequality, External Habits, and Self-Reported Happiness," AEA Papers and Proceedings, vol. 97, no. 2 (May 2007), pp. 226-231.

[15] Cahit Guven and Bent E. Sorensen, Subjective Well-Being: Keeping Up With the Joneses, Real or Perceived?, November 2007, available at http://www.uh.edu/ ~cguven/ papers/JonesesCahit_SEP262007.pdf. See also Cahit Guven and Bent E. Sorensen, "Subjective Well-Being: Keeping Up with the Perception of the Joneses," Social Indicators Research, August 2011, pp. 1-31.

In: Income Distribution in the United States ISBN: 978-1-63482-675-4
Editor: Clayton Diaz

Chapter 3

THE U.S. INCOME DISTRIBUTION AND MOBILITY: TRENDS AND INTERNATIONAL COMPARISONS*

Linda Levine

SUMMARY

The historically slow rebound in the labor market from the 2007-2009 recession appears to be partly responsible for the current focus of some within the public policy community on the unequal distribution of the benefits of economic growth (e.g., higher national income) across U.S. households. This report examines changes over time and across countries in the shape of the income distribution to afford Members of Congress a broader perspective when deliberating such policy issues as the progressivity of income tax rates, the generosity of social insurance programs, and the level of the minimum wage.

If income were equally divided across households, each quintile (fifth) of households would account for 20% of total income. Inequality is the term commonly used to describe an income distribution in which one or more quintiles account for less (more) than 20% of aggregate income. The Congressional Budget Office and others have documented that the bottom fifth has long accounted for much less than its proportionate share

* This is an edited, reformatted and augmented version of a Congressional Research Service publication R42400, prepared for Members and Committees of Congress, dated November 29, 2012.

(20%) of total income. The bottom quintile's share of income has remained little changed for the past few decades at less than 4%, according to U.S. Census Bureau data. The middle class, defined as the middle 60% of households, received a disproportionately smaller share of the total economic pie in 2011 (45.7%) than in 1968 (53.2%). Over the same period, the disproportionately large income shares of the top 20% and the top 5% of households have trended upward. The top fifth's share of total household income rose from 42.6% in 1968 to 51.1% in 2011; the top 5%'s share rose from 16.3% to 22.3%. Estimates derived from federal income tax data, which allow researchers to look within the top 5% of the U.S. income distribution, suggest that those at the very top have reaped disproportionately larger gains from economic growth. These, among other measures of income dispersion, have led analysts to conclude that inequality has increased in the United States as a result of high-income households pulling further away from those lower in the distribution.

Based on the limited data that are comparable across nations, the U.S. income distribution appears to be among the most unequal of all major industrialized countries and the United States appears to be among the nations experiencing the greatest increases in measures of income dispersion. Three leading explanations are put forth for these cross-country differences: (1) other advanced economies devote a larger share of national output to transfers, which tends to equalize income across households; (2) the progressivity of tax rates varies by country and thus has different effects on the distribution of after-tax income; and (3) equality in the distribution of earnings, which account for most household income, varies substantially across countries.

The extent to which countries undertake policies that affect their income distributions may reflect national differences in perceptions about the degree of income mobility. In the United States, a longstanding argument against redistributionary policies has been that each person has an equal opportunity to move up the income ladder. Research raises questions about whether Americans' perceptions of their likelihood of upward mobility are exaggerated. Empirical analyses estimate that the United States is a comparatively immobile society, that is, where one starts in the income distribution influences where one ends up to a greater degree than in several advanced economies. Children raised in families at the bottom of the U.S. income distribution are estimated to be especially less likely to ascend the income ladder as adults.

INTRODUCTION

The historically slow pace of recovery in the labor market from the 2007-2009 recession appears to be partly responsible for the renewed interest among some members of the public policy community in the long-term trend of growing inequality in the distribution of income.[1] In other words, the benefits of economic growth (e.g., higher national income) began accruing unequally across U.S. households long before the late 2000s. Inequality is the label commonly applied to income distributions in which a group's share of total income is larger (smaller) than its share of the population (e.g., the top 20% of U.S. households accounted for slightly more than 50% of aggregate household income in 2011, as shown in *Table 1*.)

Economic theory provides little basis for preferring any particular degree of equality in the distribution of income. In theory, what matters with respect to labor income is that the distribution results from markets that operate efficiently; that is, markets in which the final demand for goods and services and the relative productivity of the firms producing those goods and services determine the demand for labor and the earnings of jobs in each sector of the economy. Theoretical arguments for a more equal distribution of income than that which results from market forces are based on a number of propositions, including the diminishing marginal utility of income. This refers to the idea that each additional dollar of income yields less and less satisfaction (utility) than the first. For example, one additional dollar of income adds less to the utility of someone earning $100,000 than to the satisfaction of someone earning $20,000. If this proposition is correct, it should be possible to increase the overall economic well-being of society by transferring money from those with high incomes to those with low incomes because the loss in utility will be less for high-income individuals than the gain for low-income individuals. However, the costs commonly associated with income redistribution (e.g., slower economic growth) may offset some and possibly all of any net gain in well-being.[2]

With varying perceptions about a trade-off between economic growth and income equality, members of the U.S. public policy community have long debated how best to improve the economic well-being of the population. This disagreement appears to underlie longstanding congressional deliberations about several policy issues, such as the progressivity of income tax rates, tax treatment of capital gains and inheritance, provision of social insurance (e.g., Social Security) as well as social welfare benefits (e.g., food stamps), and raising the federal minimum wage. It also has extended to consideration of initiatives (e.g., grants for early childhood education and college tuition tax expenditures) that arguably promote equality in the opportunity to move up the income ladder, which an increasingly unequal distribution of income may suggest a lack of and which may itself curb the potential productive capacity of the economy.[3]

This report presents recent analysis of the distribution of income and the extent of income mobility in the United States over time and in comparison with other advanced economies. It begins with a discussion of data issues related to measuring income and its distribution. The empirical literature on the development of and explanations for income inequality in the United States are next addressed. The report then compares the U.S. income distribution with the distributions of other industrialized countries and presents explanations for cross-country differences in measures of income dispersion. To the degree that a more equal distribution of income arises from policy decisions rather than market forces, the willingness of a country to incur any economic costs related to attaining greater equality may reflect varying national beliefs about the opportunity to ascend the income ladder. For that reason, the report closes with an examination of income mobility in the United States and other developed nations.

MEASURES OF INCOME

Two common sources of income data are the Annual Social and Economic supplement to the Current Population Survey (CPS) and federal income tax returns submitted to the Internal Revenue Service (IRS). The U.S. Census Bureau, which conducts the CPS, calculates "money income." It is the nation's official measure of income. Money income includes wages and salaries, interest, dividends, rent, payments from pensions and retirement savings accounts, and nonmeans-tested cash income (e.g., Social Security, unemployment compensation, and veterans' payments). Calculated on a pre-tax basis, money income does not include the value of noncash government benefits (e.g., food stamps and housing subsidies) and capital gains.[4]

"Market income" is the measure of income derived from federal tax data made available by the IRS. Perhaps most prominent among the researchers who use tax data to study the distribution of income are Saez and Piketty. They define pre-tax market income to include all income reported on individual tax returns including wages and salaries, business and farm income, and capital income (e.g., dividends, interest, and rents).[5] The primary differences between money and market income thus defined is that market income excludes cash government benefits and includes realized capital gains.

With respect to the distribution of overall economic well-being, measures based on the concepts of money and market income fall short and may be misleading. Consider the case of two families who in every way are equal in terms of wealth and income. Neither owns their home, and they both have substantial savings in interest-earning assets. Suppose one family uses a portion of its savings to buy a home. No one would argue that the family is now worse off, but income measures indicate that to be the case because the family's interest income would have fallen. In fact, the family that buys its home is earning an implicit income in the use of the house just as it would earn rental income if the house were leased to others.

Another weakness in existing income measures as a reflection of overall economic well-being is that they do not account for the implicit income of homemakers. Consider two married-couple households with the same income and both spouses receive wages from their employers. If in one of the households a spouse quits to stay at home and care for their children that household will experience a drop in measured income. Because the unpaid work done at home is not without value, the measured difference in the incomes of the two households will overstate the difference in their living standards.

The time period in which income is measured may also affect comparisons in well-being across households. Over the course of the business cycle unemployment rises and falls, affecting labor income. Some households tend to be more adversely affected than others by recessions, so the stage of the business cycle has an influence on relative income. Similarly, income generally varies substantially over the course of an individual's lifetime. New entrants to the labor force typically have lower incomes than those who have been working for some time, and income tends to decrease upon retirement. Because of these life-cycle changes in income, the age mix of the population also influences the relative incomes of households.

Another difficulty in comparing income across households is deciding on the relevant population. In the case of labor income, the distribution of income among working-age individuals (e.g., 25- 64-year olds) may be of most interest. When it comes to overall well-being, it may be more appropriate to consider the distribution of income across households. Because most households can be presumed to pool resources and because some costs of living are fixed, a four-person household may not need twice as much income as a married-couple household for each person to enjoy roughly the same living standard.[6] The ability to achieve economies of scale thus further complicates using the distribution of income across households or tax filing units as a basis for judging economic well-being.[7]

Measures of the Distribution of Income

The Census Bureau annually publishes a variety of measures that describe the distribution of money income. One measure divides total money income into quintiles (fifths), with households ordered from lowest to highest income and then divided into five groups of equal size. The income within each group is summed, and its share (percentage) of total household income is calculated. If aggregate income was equally divided across households with income, each quintile would account for 20% of total money income. To the extent that each quintile falls short of or exceeds its proportionate (20%) share, it indicates the degree of inequality in the income distribution.

As shown in the last row of *Table 1*, the bottom fifth of households in 2011 accounted for much less than the one-fifth of total income it would have gotten if the distribution were perfectly equal. The top 20%, in contrast, accounted for more than twice what it would have gotten in an equal distribution. The top 5%, which is within the top fifth, accounted for more than four times the share it would have had in a perfectly equal distribution. The data thus indicate that income was quite unequally distributed across U.S. households in 2011, and that this has been the case for quite some time.

Households at various points in the distribution also have fared differently from each other over the past few decades. Between 1968 and 2011, the income share of the three middle quintiles fell from 53.2% to 45.7% (see Table 1). Although there is no official definition of the middle class, the middle 60% of households is sometimes regarded as such.[8] As for the bottom 20% of households, its income share has stagnated at less than 4.0% since about 1990. In contrast, the income shares of the top fifth and the top 5% of households generally have risen from year to year. The top 20%'s share grew from 42.6% in 1968 to 51.1% in 2011, and the top 5%'s share grew from 16.3% to 22.3%.

Another indicator of the degree of inequality is the Gini coefficient. It is a single number that can range between zero (a perfectly equal distribution) and one (a perfectly unequal distribution).[9] The historical trend in the United States is one of almost steadily increasing income inequality (from 0.386 in 1968 to 0.477 in 2011), as depicted in *Figure 1*. During the 2007-2009 recession, the Gini coefficient fell slightly from its previous peak in 2006 of 0.470. Its level since then indicates an income distribution that is much more unequal than in most years since 1968.

Table 1. Distribution of U.S. Household Income by Quintile, Selected Years (1968-2011)

Year	Percentage of Total Household Income					
	Bottom	Second	Third	Fourth	Fifth	Top 5%
1968	4.2	11.1	17.6	24.5	42.6	16.3
1980	4.2	10.2	16.8	24.7	44.1	16.5
1990	3.8	9.6	15.9	24.0	46.6	18.5
2000	3.6	8.9	14.8	23.0	49.8	22.1
2001	3.5	8.7	14.6	23.0	50.1	22.4
2002	3.5	8.8	14.8	23.3	49.7	21.7
2003	3.4	8.7	14.8	23.4	49.8	21.4
2004	3.4	8.7	14.7	23.2	50.1	21.8
2005	3.4	8.6	14.6	23.0	50.4	22.2
2006	3.4	8.6	14.5	22.9	50.5	22.3
2007	3.4	8.7	14.8	23.4	49.7	21.2
2008	3.4	8.6	14.7	23.3	50.0	21.5
2009	3.4	8.6	14.6	23.2	50.3	21.7
2010	3.3	8.5	14.6	23.4	50.3	21.3
2011	3.2	8.4	14.3	23.0	51.1	22.3

Source: U.S. Census Bureau, Table A-2 of Income, Poverty, and Health Insurance Coverage in the United States: 2011.

Researchers who work with the CPS data often calculate an alternative measure of overall inequality (the ratio of income at the 90th percentile in the distribution to income at the 10th percentile) because the Gini coefficient does not allow them to ascertain which parts of the income distribution are driving changes in inequality. An increase in the ratio of the median income level (50th percentile) to the 10th percentile income level (the 50-10 ratio) suggests that growth in overall inequality (the 90-10 ratio) is due to those near the bottom of the distribution falling further behind the typical household. An increase in the ratio of the 90th percentile to the median income level (the 90-50 ratio) suggests that growth in overall inequality is due to those near the top of the distribution pulling further ahead of the typical household. Based on these measures, increased inequality in the upper half of the distribution may have accounted for most of the overall increase in inequality between 1961 and 2002.[10] Looking at just the 1990-2002 period, almost all of the increase in overall inequality appears to be due to an increase in top-half inequality. This pattern of the benefits of economic growth accruing largely to those near the top of the income distribution was estimated to have continued through 2007.[11]

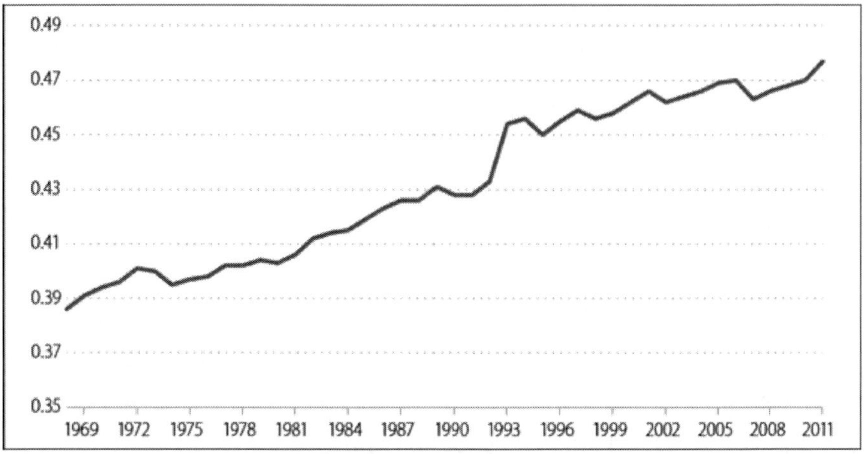

Source: Created by CRS from data in Table A-2 of the U.S. Census Bureau's Income, Poverty, and Health Insurance Coverage: 2011.

Notes: The sharp increase in the Gini coefficient in the early 1990s was due to the redesign of the CPS.

Figure 1. Gini Coefficients for U.S. Households, 1968-2011.

The 90-10 ratio may be a poor substitute for estimating overall inequality at a point in time and over time because it is affected by top-coding in the CPS. Top-coding refers to the Census Bureau's long-standing practice of replacing the income reported above a specific level with that income level to ensure confidentiality. For example, if the total money income of a household was $780,000 in 2011, the household's income would have been coded as $250,000 because $250,000 was the threshold income level in that year. Top-coding therefore presents a problem when estimating the extent of inequality in a given year because it constrains the actual distribution of income. The practice also creates a problem when estimating changes in inequality over time because the top-code thresholds were raised at various times over the years and as a result, the share of households with suppressed incomes has differed over time.[12]

These drawbacks to using CPS data, in combination with anecdotal evidence that since the 1990s those in the top 10% have pulled further away from other households, prompted economists to turn to other data sources that better capture those with high incomes. Piketty and Saez developed a time series from the early years of the 20th century forward based primarily on federal income tax returns to study changes in market income among tax units at the very top of the income distribution.[13] They estimated that between 40% and 45% of total income accrued to the top 10% of the distribution between the two World Wars before falling to about 30% during World War II. The top decile's share remained at 31%-32% until the 1970s when it began trending upward. The top decile's share again exceeded 40% by the mid-1990s and has been at all-time highs in recent years. In 2010, the latest year for which an estimate is available, the top 10% accounted for over 46% of aggregate market income.[14]

Piketty and Saez attribute most of the changes in the top decile's share over time to fluctuations in the top 1% of the distribution. They estimated that before World War I the top 1% accounted for about 18% of total market income. Its share peaked at almost 24% in the late 1920s, fell to about 8% from the late 1950s to the 1970s, and then turned upward.[15] The top 1% was estimated to have accounted for over 17% of total market income in 2010, about equal to its pre-World War I share.[16]

Like the CPS, tax returns have limitations for analyzing income inequality (e.g., time-shifting income through use of deferred compensation, such as stock options, and reporting income as earnings or business profits depending on their tax treatment in a given year). Burkhauser, Feng, Jenkins et al. attempted to reconcile the smaller increases in money income inequality starting in the 1990s that are estimated by studies based on public-use CPS data with the larger increases in market income inequality of studies based on tax data. Using internal Census Bureau data (which is less subject to top-coding than is public-use data) to estimate income shares of those in the 90th-95th percentile, the 95th-99th percentile, and the top 1%, they found that inequality trends during most of the 1967-2006 period were quite similar to those of studies that used tax data once comparable definitions of income and income-receiving units were employed.[17]

Burkhauser, Larrimore, and Simon more recently estimated that if after-tax, after-transfer income adjusted for household size is analyzed rather than before-tax, before-transfer income of tax units

> income inequality in the United States increased [between 1979 and 2007] not because the rich got richer, the poor got poorer and the middle class stagnated, but because the rich got richer at a faster rate than the middle and poorer quintiles and this mainly occurred in the 1980s. [Absolute as opposed to relative income] growth was substantial in all quintiles once the influence of government tax and

> transfer policy as well as the shift in compensation from wages to health insurance provided by employers and the shift to increased in-kind health insurance by government is more fully recognized.[18]

A Congressional Budget Office report also examined after-tax, after-transfer size-adjusted household income over the 1979-2007 period. It too estimated that absolute levels of inflation-adjusted average household income increased across the distribution, but because the rate of increase was much greater among the highest income households, inequality increased after 1979. For example, the top 1% of households saw their average real income rise by 275% from 1979 to 2007; the middle three quintiles experienced a 37% increase; and the bottom fifth recorded an 18% gain. Consequently, in 2007, the share of income after taxes and transfers of the top 20% of size-adjusted households was greater than the combined share of the other 80% of households (58% and 47%, respectively).[19]

EXPLAINING RECENT TRENDS IN THE DISTRIBUTION OF U.S. HOUSEHOLD INCOME

Two explanations are most commonly offered for the trend toward greater inequality in the distribution of labor income in the United States.[20] One has to do with globalization, that is, the increased integration of countries' economies. The second relates to the nature of recent technological advances.

Reduced trade restrictions and increased worldwide flows of goods and services have arguably made less skilled U.S. workers in particular more vulnerable to direct competition from less skilled workers abroad. In theory, the shift overseas in production of goods and services that predominantly use less-skilled workers has reduced demand in the United States for these workers, thereby putting downward pressure on their wages and further widening the existing wage gap between lower and higher skilled U.S. workers.

Economists generally have not agreed about globalization being a major contributor to increasing income inequality because little compelling empirical evidence supports the theory. Analyses of globalization's employment effect to date have tended to find it too small to explain the magnitude of the earnings gap. Other studies have estimated that many jobs possess characteristics which make them susceptible to being offshored and that they are not limited to low-skilled jobs.[21] As it is technological advances (e.g., high-speed telecommunication) that have made these jobs (e.g., call center workers) vulnerable to offshore outsourcing, some have suggested that globalization cannot be separated from the technological change argument (discussed below).[22]

Economists generally have found technological change to be the most persuasive explanation for increased inequality at the top of the earnings distribution.[23] Frequently cited evidence underlying this explanation is the comparatively rapid growth in the wage premium paid to more highly skilled (productive) workers since 1979. The increase in the "skill premium" coincided with substantial growth in the percentage of the labor force with a college education. This suggests that the growth in their supply did not keep pace with the increase in employer demand for highly skilled workers.[24]

The increased premium paid to high-skilled workers is commonly ascribed to the nature of technological change in recent decades. Put another way, the kinds of technological advances that have occurred since the late 1970s have been biased in favor of those jobs that require higher levels of education and training. Technological progress seemingly has affected the earnings distribution in two ways. First, information technology (IT) serves as a substitute for low-skilled workers, which has reduced demand for and the relative wages of these workers. Second, IT serves as a complement to high-skilled workers, which has raised demand for and the relative wages of these workers.[25] Autor, Katz, and Kearney have refined this explanation. They hypothesize that computerization of tasks has polarized the labor market by

- increasing employer demand for those high-skilled workers who perform non-routine cognitive tasks (e.g., engineers and lawyers);
- keeping demand stable for those low-skilled workers who perform non-routine manual tasks (e.g., truck drivers and home health care aides); and
- decreasing demand for the many medium-skilled workers who perform routine tasks (e.g., administrative support and factory workers).

They estimated that this pattern of job growth has produced substantial earnings gains among workers in the top quartile (25%) of the distribution. Workers in the bottom quartile were found to have experienced slower gains than workers in the top quartile. Nonetheless, wage growth of the bottom quartile appears to have exceeded that of workers in the middle of the earnings distribution.[26]

Two less often mentioned explanations for the increase in U.S. income inequality are the declining role of labor unions and labor standards in wage-setting and the changing demographics of the population. Some analysts have offered evidence of inconsistencies in the data that do not support the skill-biased technological change (SBTC) explanation[27] and have argued that changes over time in economic institutions and social norms have played a part as well (e.g., the value of the federal minimum wage and the bargaining power of labor unions).[28] Others have examined changes over time in the U.S. age structure, racial and ethnic composition, and household living arrangements (e.g., away from married-couple families and toward single adult households).[29]

International Comparisons of Income Distributions

Cross-country comparisons of income distributions provide another perspective on the extent of inequality in the United States. Measures of income differ from one country to the next. For this reason, researchers typically use data made more comparable by the Luxembourg Income Study (LIS) project or by the Organisation for Economic Cooperation and Development (OECD).[30]

Researchers who analyzed LIS data from the mid-1970s to 2000 agree that the comparatively high level of inequality in the United States has been in place for quite some time and that the United States was among those countries that experienced the largest increases in inequality over the 25-year period.[31] They found the most equal distributions of disposable household income over the lengthy period were in Scandinavia, Central Europe and Southern Europe, while most English-speaking countries consistently had the highest levels of inequality. Between the mid-1970s and 2000, Sweden, Finland, and Norway appear to have experienced the smallest increases in inequality, whereas the United States, the United Kingdom, and Italy seemingly experienced the largest increases. The United States also was estimated to have had the most persistent increase in inequality from the mid-1970s to 2000, whereas the rate at which inequality increased in other industrialized nations generally slowed in the later years of the period.

LIS income distribution measures for the mid-2000s for several industrialized nations are presented in *Table 2*.

Table 2. Summary Measures of Disposable Household Income Distributions for Selected Countries in the Mid-2000s

Country	Year	Gini Coefficient	P_{90}/P_{10}	P_{90}/P_{50}
Denmark	2004	0.228	2.778	1.562
Slovenia	2004	0.231	2.920	1.650
Sweden	2005	0.237	2.821	1.625
Finland	2004	0.256	3.071	1.708
Norway	2004	0.256	2.865	1.604
Netherlands	2004	0.266	3.018	1.737
Austria	2004	0.269	3.232	1.787
Germany	2004	0.278	3.445	1.823
France	2005	0.280	3.528	1.842
Australia	2003	0.312	4.241	1.983
Poland	2004	0.315	4.022	1.959
Canada	2004	0.318	4.379	1.957
Greece	2004	0.327	4.374	2.027
Italy	2004	0.340	4.440	2.029
United Kingdom	2004	0.344	4.411	2.137
United States	2004	0.370	5.506	2.126
Mexico	2004	0.457	8.468	2.945
Colombia	2004	0.506	11.254	3.334

Source: LIS, Inequality Key Figures, http://www.lisdatacenter.org.

Note: Disposable household income is market income (e.g., earnings, self-employment income, pensions, rent, and dividends) plus public transfer payments (e.g., old-age and unemployment insurance, maternity and family support) less personal income tax payments and workers' social security contributions, adjusted for size of household.

The countries are listed in order from lowest Gini coefficient (most equal distribution) to highest (most unequal distribution). According to this measure, the United States (after-tax after cash transfers) household income in the mid-2000s. The comparatively high degree of income inequality in the United States is evident from the 90-10 and 90-50 ratios as well. As indicated by the 90-10 ratio, those at the top of the U.S. income distribution had more than five times the income of those near the bottom. Those at the top of the U.S. distribution also had about twice the income of the typical household, as indicated by the 90-50 ratio.

With virtually no change between the mid and late 2000s in the ranking of countries by extent of inequality in disposable household income, the United

States was again among the nations with the most unequal distributions (see Gini coefficients in *Table 2* and *Table 3*).[32] U.S. income inequality in the late 2000s surpassed the average for the 20 founding member countries of the OECD (see *Table 3*).

Table 3. Summary Measure of Disposable Household Income Distributions for Selected Countries in the Late 2000s and Change from Mid-1980s to Late 2000s

		Percentile Point Change	
Country	*Gini Coefficienta*	*Mid-1980s to Mid-1990s*	*Mid-1990s to Late 2000s*
Slovenia	0.236	n.a.	n.a.
Denmark	0.248	-0.6	3.3
Norway	0.25	2.1	0.7
Finland	0.259	2.1	3.2
Sweden	0.259	1.4	4.8
Austria	0.261	n.a.	2.7
France	0.293	-2.3	1.6
Netherlands	0.294	2.5	-0.3
Germany	0.295	1.5	3.0
Poland	0.305	n.a.	n.a.
Greece	0.307	0.0	-2.8
Canada	0.324	-0.4	3.5
Australia	0.336	n.a.	2.7
Italy	0.337	3.9	-1.1
United Kingdom	0.345	2.7	0.9
United States	0.378	2.3	1.8
Mexico	0.476	6.6	-4.3
Chile	0.494	n.a.	-3.3
OECD20b	0.316	2.1	0.5

Source: OECD, Divided We Stand: Why Inequality Keeps Rising, December 5, 2011, p. 45.

Notes: Disposable household income is market income (e.g., earnings, self-employment income, pensions, rent, and dividends) plus public transfer payments (e.g., old-age and unemployment insurance, maternity and family support) less personal income tax payments and workers' social security contributions, adjusted for size of household. n.a. = not available.

[a] The Gini coefficients are for 2008, except for Chile (2009) and Denmark (2007).

[b] The OECD20 are the founding countries: Austria, Belgium, Canada, Denmark, France, Germany, Greece, Iceland, Ireland, Italy, Luxembourg, Netherlands, Norway, Portugal, Spain, Sweden, Switzerland, Turkey, the United Kingdom, and the United States.

Disposable household income inequality in the developed countries of the OECD, including those listed in *Table 3*, has generally trended upward since the mid-1980s.[33] While inequality in the United States increased by slightly more than the OECD20 average during the mid-1980s to mid-1990s period, the increase in U.S. inequality was considerably greater relative to the OECD average from the mid-1990s to late 2000s (see the last columns of *Table 3*).

EXPLAINING CROSS-COUNTRY DIFFERENCES IN THE DISTRIBUTION OF INCOME

Reasons commonly offered for international differences in income inequality fall into three categories. First, many other countries devote a much larger share of their national output (gross domestic product, GDP) to income transfers, which have an equalizing effect on the distribution of income. Second, taxes in these countries vary with respect to progressivity, and thus have different effects on the distribution of after-tax income. Third, equality in the distribution of earnings, which make up the majority of household income, varies substantially from one country to another.

Smeeding estimated a strong correlation between the income share of those at the low end of the distribution and the share of GDP accounted for by transfer payments. His analysis suggests that given the amount of money transferred to households in the United States and the United Kingdom, those at the low end of their respective income distributions do not benefit as much from transfers as low-income households in other countries. From this Smeeding concluded that transfer payments are not as well targeted at low-income households in the United States as they are in many other nations.[34]

The OECD estimated that public cash transfers and household taxes (i.e., income tax payments and social security contributions) substantially reduce inequality between market income and disposable income. These government policies were found to have lowered income inequality by one-fourth on average in the mid-2000s. The redistributive effect of public cash transfers and household taxes was smaller than average in the United States. While transfer payments were found to have reduced inequality by twice as much as taxes on average in OECD countries, the opposite was true in the United States; that is, income tax payments and social security contributions were more responsible than government cash transfers for reducing inequality in the United States.[35]

This pattern was confirmed in a study of 36 developed and developing countries that are in the LIS database. Wang and Caminada estimated that "taxes are important in equalizing incomes" in only four countries: the United States, Canada, Israel, and Guatemala.[36] Whereas they found that, compared with the other countries analyzed, social transfers make up a low percentage of the U.S. budget and are not as well targeted at those at the bottom of the income distribution; the researchers suggest that the refundable Earned Income Tax Credit (EITC) "makes the US tax system rather progressive."[37]

Others note that in the United States the relative contributions of transfers and taxes to reducing income inequality changed over time, with cash assistance to those at the bottom of the distribution reduced after passage of the Personal Responsibility and Work Opportunity Reconciliation Act of 1996 (popularly known as welfare reform), while the value of the EITC increased greatly.[38] It nonetheless appears that changes in the federal tax system through 2006 (including the EITC and the refundable child tax credit) little affected the rising trend in U.S. household income inequality.[39]

When in-kind benefits (e.g., health insurance, education, child and elder care) and indirect taxes (e.g., sales, value-added and property) are taken into account, cross-country differences in inequality at the low end of the distribution are reduced. This again points to the importance of the definition of income when estimating inequality. Garfinkel, Rainwater, and Smeeding estimated that in the United States cash transfers to those at the bottom of the income distribution are comparatively small while in-kind benefits are substantial.[40]

Differences between countries' labor market institutions and policies appear to affect the shape of the earnings distribution, particularly for those in the bottom half. It has been suggested that the more centralized or coordinated process of wage-setting in several countries (e.g., Germany) helps to explain the wage compression toward the bottom of their earnings distributions compared with that of the United States.[41] This may be due, in part, to higher private sector unionization rates in some other industrialized countries and a larger share of their workers being affected by union agreements whether or not they are union members. The decrease in union density in the United States and United Kingdom between 1973 and 1998 may have accounted for 3% of the increase in male wage inequality in the United States and 5% in the United Kingdom, for example.[42] Comparatively greater union bargaining power (or higher minimum wages) also may have caused firms in other countries to pay low skilled workers wage rates above their contribution to output.[43] This, in turn, may have prompted these foreign companies to adopt technologies that raised the productivity of their less skilled employees rather than adopt technologies biased in favor of high skilled workers as has occurred in the United States.

INCOME MOBILITY IN THE UNITED STATES

To the extent that greater equality in the distribution of income results from policy decisions about taxes and transfers, for example, and not from market forces, that equality may have been achieved at some cost (e.g., slower economic growth). Assuming the costs are recognized, the willingness to incur them may reflect varying degrees of concern across countries about income inequality. The results of a study that compared the relationship between individuals' perceptions of their well-being and the extent of inequality in the United States and Europe suggest that inequality in the distribution of income is less important to people in the United States due to Americans believing that they live in a comparatively mobile society.[44] That is to say, Americans may be less concerned about inequality in the distribution of income at any given point in time partly because of a belief that everyone has an equal opportunity to move up the income ladder. A review of the literature suggests that Americans' perceptions about their likelihood of changing position in the income distribution may be exaggerated.

Intergenerational Mobility

Intergenerational elasticity (IGE) measures how persistent position in the income distribution is from one generation to the next. IGE is a single number that indicates the extent to which parents' position in the income distribution explains their adult children's relative income. The lower the elasticity, the less likely inequality is to be perpetuated from one generation to the next; that is, the more mobile the society.

Empirical analyses have estimated a strong positive relationship—about 0.5—between parent and adult child income in the United States.[45] An IGE of 0.5 suggests that if the income of a child's parents was 30% higher than the average income of families in the parents' generation, then the child's income will be 15% above the average for his/her generation. In other words, in the United States, about 50% of the (dis)advantage of growing up in a (low) high income family may be inherited.

The Trend in Intergenerational Mobility in the United States

It is difficult to precisely answer the question of whether the importance of parents' relative income to adult children's relative income changed over the period that inequality has been increasing in the United States. This is partly the case because few sources cover multiple generations of adults for which data are available on family income at the time they were children. As described more fully below, empirical analyses suggest that children born into low-income families have not become more likely and may have become less likely to surpass their parents' position at the bottom of the income distribution. Put differently, mobility in the United States does not appear to have offset the increase in cross-sectional inequality in recent decades.

Lee and Solon used data from the Panel Study of Income Dynamics (PSID) for children born between 1952 and 1975 who reached age 25 between 1977 and 2000 to estimate IGEs. They found no major change during the two decades in the influence of parent income on adult sons' incomes. The IGE in each year was estimated to be within 0.1 percentage point of the 0.44 average over the 1980s and 1990s.[46] Hertz, who also relied on the PSID but used a variety of estimation methods, similarly found no substantial change in mobility among cohorts of male and female children born between 1952 and 1975 when observed as adults starting in the late 1970s.[47]

Levine and Mazumder used an entirely different methodology than the aforementioned economists whose research also was based on longitudinal data. Levine and Mazumder examined the incomes of brothers from two cohorts in the National Longitudinal Surveys (NLS). The older group was composed of brothers who entered the labor market during the 1970s; the younger group, brothers who entered the labor market between the early 1980s and mid-1990s. They estimated that family background, as represented by correlations between sibling incomes, was more important to the economic outcomes of the younger cohort (which entered the workforce after 1980).[48] Specifically, the correlation between brothers' incomes doubled from 0.21 for the older group to 0.42 for the younger group. From this marked increase in the correlation, Levine and Mazumder infer that intergenerational mobility decreased substantially at some point between 1983 and 1995.[49]

Aaronson and Mazumder took yet another approach because they used decennial census data which, although it allowed them to cover a longer period, does not follow the same individuals over time as do the PSID and NLS.[50] They estimated that movement between generations from one part of the income distribution to another increased over the 1940-1980 period. Intergenerational mobility then decreased substantially during the 1980s and appears to have remained unchanged during the 1990s. This pattern suggests that the opportunity for children in the United States to attain incomes that exceed their parents' relative incomes was lower after 1980 compared to the preceding four decades.[51] In a more recent article, Mazumder concluded that his research with Aaronson "and the studies using the PSID are in broad agreement that intergenerational mobility has been roughly flat since 1990."[52]

Cross-Country Comparisons of Intergenerational Mobility

Analysts have developed estimates of intergenerational mobility that use differing statistical approaches and are based on the longitudinal surveys and administrative records available in each country. The cross-country estimates usually are derived from earnings of fathers and their adult sons because data on daughters and other sources of income are more limited in countries other than the United States. Although the rank of the United States differs somewhat from one study to the next, as discussed below, the United States typically is found to be among the least mobile of the advanced economies.

Corak reviewed numerous studies that offered differing estimates of intergenerational earnings persistence for each of several advanced economies. Based on his assessment of the preferred IGE for the nations in the meta-analysis, Corak concluded that the United Kingdom, the United States, and France are the least mobile. In these countries, about 41% (France) to 50% (United Kingdom) of the economic advantage high-earning young men have over lower earners may be due to their coming from more affluent families. In the cases of Canada, Finland, Norway, and Denmark, the effect of fathers' on adult sons' relative earnings was found to be lower (about 20% or less). With IGEs of about 30%, mobility in Germany and Sweden falls between these two groups.[53]

Studies of intergenerational economic mobility in southern European countries have less often been undertaken due partly to a paucity of long panels that enable comparison of the income of fathers and their adult children. In a recent study that was designed to overcome data limitations, Cervini-Pia estimated an income elasticity of 0.40 for sons and about the same for daughters in Spain—making it less mobile than many of the advanced economies discussed above but more mobile than the United States (which in Corak's review had a preferred IGE of 0.47).[54] Piraino estimated an intergenerational earnings elasticity of 0.435 and an income elasticity of 0.554 for Italy, "which indicates that about one-half of the economic advantage of Italian fathers is passed on to their sons."[55] Mocetti developed higher elasticities for Italy than Piranio, at about 0.50 for earnings and 0.61 for income. Both sets of estimates for Italy suggest that it is less economically mobile than the United States.

Jantti et al. developed intergenerational samples for six countries from which they derived estimates of intergenerational mobility at different points in the joint distribution of father and son earnings. The estimation of transition matrices allowed them to compare mobility rates from one quintile to another in the distribution. The researchers found that the United States has less upward mobility from the bottom quintile and more low-income persistence than the United Kingdom and Nordic countries (Denmark, Finland, Norway, and Sweden) included in their analysis. More specifically, between 20% and 30% of children whose fathers were in the bottom fifth of the earnings distributions remained at the bottom as adults, but for the United States, about 40% of children stayed in the bottom fifth. The authors suggest that, despite these results, Americans have been able to maintain the perception of living in a mobile society because transition rates of the middle three quintiles are similar in the United States and other advanced economies. "In the U.S., such middle class moves are associated with fairly substantial changes in real living standards (i.e., measured in actual dollars earned) ... [that] are experienced or witnessed by a substantial fraction of the U.S. population."[56]

A recent study by the Pew Economic Mobility Project (EMP) lends support to Jantti et al.'s estimate of low upward mobility from the bottom fifth of the U.S. income distribution. The analysis found that 43% of children whose parents were in the bottom quintile remained in the bottom as adults. The EMP also estimated that children raised by parents in the top quintile tended to be in the top quintile as adults (40%). In contrast, children raised by parents in the three middle quintiles (the middle class) experienced much higher rates of mobility: only 25% of children born to parents in the second fifth were in the same place as adults; only 14% of children whose parents were in the middle fifth stayed in the middle fifth as adults; and only 9% of children raised by parents in the fourth quintile were in the same relative position as adults.[57]

Intragenerational Mobility

Much the same results are evident when it comes to intragenerational mobility in the United States. The likelihood of adults moving from their initial positions in the income distribution has decreased or been unchanged in recent decades, according to available empirical analyses.

Bradbury used data from the PSID to analyze family income mobility for working-age married couples over the 1969-2006 period. The various measures of mobility she developed indicate that family income mobility declined between 1969 and 2006, and particularly since the 1980s. Families, whether they started at the bottom or top of the income distribution, became increasingly less likely to move up or down the income ladder during their working lives. Bradbury concluded that "family income mobility has been insufficient to stem increases in inequality of long-term income."[58]

Acs and Zimmerman used PSID data to determine the trend in income mobility among 25-44- year olds between 1989 and 2004. They estimated that intragenerational mobility among young adults has been stable since the 1980s. For example, slightly over one-half of 25-44-year olds were in the lowest quintile of the income distribution in both the 1984-1994 and 1994-2004 periods. About one-fourth of those in the bottom quintile moved up to the second quintile in the 1984-1994 period, the same share also moved up in the following 10-year period. Similarly, in both 1984-1994 and 1994-2004, about 10% of those in the bottom quintile were able to move into the middle quintile of the income distribution; 7%, to the fourth quintile; and 4%, to the top quintile. Mobility rates from the higher quintiles into the bottom quintile also were little changed over time: 20%-22% of those in the second quintile were downwardly mobile in the 1984-1994 and 1994-2004 periods, whereas 11%-15% of those in the middle quintile fell to the bottom quintile; 6%-7% from the fourth quintile dropped to the bottom as did 3%-4% from the top quintile. These patterns led Acs and Zimmerman to conclude that "in the context of rising income inequality, stable mobility rates suggest that the distribution of lifetime income must be growing unequal. That is, lifetime or long-term economic inequality is rising."[59]

Auten and Gee used panel data from income tax returns to examine mobility over the past two decades among tax units aged 25 and older. They similarly found that mobility was about the same in most income quintiles between the 1987-1996 and 1996-2005 periods. Auten and Gee also estimated a slight decrease in overall mobility, with 58.3% of individuals changing quintiles in 1987-1996 compared with 57.5% in 1996-2005. They found that the entire difference resulted from less downward mobility out of the top 20%.[60]

Diaz-Gimenez et al. used PSID data to analyze household income mobility between the 1989- 1994 (five-year) and 2001-2007 (six-year) periods. They estimated that income mobility was little changed, but the six-year span of the more recent period suggested a decrease in mobility.[61] DiazGimenez et al. also found less income mobility among households at the bottom and top of the income distribution compared with households in the middle three quintiles. As suggested above by Jantti with regard to cross-country intergenerational mobility, the comparatively high intragenerational mobility of a majority of U.S. households (the middle 60%) may partly account for the seeming misperception among Americans that the United States is a very mobile society.

Burkhauser and Couch reviewed the limited literature on intragenerational mobility in the United States and several other countries (e.g., the United Kingdom, Germany, France, Denmark, and Sweden). Their meta-analysis led them to conclude that there does not appear to be a clear relationship between the extent of income inequality and intragenerational income mobility. In addition, most of the studies found that the majority of cross-sectional (short-term) inequality appears to persist over time.[62]

CONCLUSION

Measures of income dispersion show a distribution of income across U.S. households that has become comparatively more unequal over time as high-income U.S. households have benefitted disproportionately from economic growth and that is less equal compared with distributions in many other developed countries. It also appears that going from rags to riches is relatively rare; that is, where one starts in the U.S. income distribution greatly influences where one ends up.

End Notes

1 D.B. Grusky and C. Wimer, "Is There Too Much Inequality?," in The Inequality Puzzle: European and US Leaders Discuss Rising Income Inequality, ed. Roland Berger, David Grusky, Tobias Raffel, Geoffrey Samuels, and Christopher Wimer (Germany: Springer, 2010), pp. 4-5.

2 For additional information, see "Reducing Income Inequality While Boosting Economic Growth: Can It Be Done?" (part II, chapter 5 of Economic Policy Reforms, Going for Growth 2012, February 2012, 200 pp.), in which the OECD identifies the impact of various policies on both growth and inequality.

3 See, for example, Florence Jaumotte, Subir Lall, and Chris Papageorgiou, Rising Income Inequality: Technology, or Trade and Financial Globalization, International Monetary Fund, Working Paper 08/185, July 1, 2008.

4 The Census Bureau also periodically calculates alternative measures of income that include such income sources as government noncash benefits and capital gains. The latest

alternative measures of income are available at http://www.census.gov/hhes/www/cpstables/032009/rdcall/1_001.htm.

[5] Thomas Piketty and Emmanuel Saez, "Income Inequality in the United States, 1913-1998," Quarterly Journal of Economics, vol. 118, no. 1 (2003), pp. 1-39. (Hereinafter referred to as Piketty and Saez, Income Inequality in the United States, 1913-1998.)

[6] In the Current Population Survey (CPS), a household is defined as all of the individuals who occupy a housing unit as their usual place of residence. A family is defined as a group of two or more individuals who reside together and who are related by birth, marriage, or adoption. A household may be composed of one or more families or no families at all; that is, a person living alone in a housing unit is counted as a household in the CPS.

[7] A tax unit is anyone who files a federal income tax return.

[8] CRS Report RS20811, The Distribution of Household Income and the Middle Class, by Linda Levine.

[9] For additional information on the Gini coefficient see Malte Luebker, Inequality, Income Shares and Poverty: the Practical Meaning of Gini Coefficients, International Labour Office, Travail Policy Brief No. 3, Geneva, Switzerland, June 2010, 8 pp.

[10] Kevin A. Bryan and Leonardo Martinez, "On the Evolution of Income Inequality in the United States," Economic Quarterly, Federal Reserve Bank of Richmond, spring 2008.

[11] Javier Diaz-Gimenez, Jose-Victor Rios-Rull, and Andy Glover, "Facts on the Distributions of Earnings, Income, and Wealth in the United States: 2007 Update," Federal Reserve Bank of Minneapolis Quarterly Review, vol. 34, no. 1 (February 2011), pp. 2-31. (Hereinafter referred to as Diaz-Gimenez et al., Facts on the Distribution of Earnings, Income, and Wealth.)

[12] Richard V. Burkhauser, Shuaizhang Feng, and Stephen P. Jenkins, "Using the P90/P10 Ratio to Measure US Inequality Trends with Current Population Survey Data: A View from Inside the Census Bureau Vaults," Review of Income and Wealth, vol. 55, no. 1 (2009), pp. 166-185.

[13] They define tax units to be married-couples living together or single adults with or without dependents in Piketty and Saez, Income Inequality in the United States, 1913-1998.

[14] Facundo Alvaredo, Anthony B. Atkinson, Thomas Piketty, and Emmanuel Saez, The World Top Income Database, http://g-mond.parisschoolofeconomics.eu/topincomes/. (Hereinafter referred to as Alvaredo, Atkinson, Piketty, and Saez, http://g-mond.parisschoolofeconomics.eu/topincomes/.)

[15] Piketty and Saez, Income Inequality in the United States, 1913-1998.

[16] Alvaredo, Atkinson, Piketty, and Saez, http://g-mond.parisschoolofeconomics.eu/topincomes/.

[17] Richard V. Burkhauser, Shuaizhang Feng, and Stephen P. Jenkins et al., Recent Trends in Top Income Shares in the USA: Reconciling Estimates from the March CPS and IRS Tax Return Data, National Bureau of Economic Research (NBER), Working Paper 15320, Cambridge, MA, September 2009.

[18] Richard V. Burkhauser, Jeff Larrimore, and Kosali I. Simon, A "Second Opinion" on the Economic Health of the American Middle Class, NBER, Working Paper 17164, Cambridge, MA, June 2011, p. 21.

[19] Congressional Budget Office, Trends in the Distribution of Household Income between 1979 and 2007, Washington, DC, October 2011.

[20] Labor income is the leading contributor to household income, according to the Survey of Consumer Finances sponsored by the Federal Reserve Board.

[21] CRS Report RL32292, Offshoring (or Offshore Outsourcing) and Job Loss Among U.S. Workers, by Linda Levine.

[22] Richard B. Freeman, "Globalization and Inequality," in The Oxford Handbook of Economic Inequality, ed. Wiemer Salverda, Brian Nolan, and Timothy M. Smeeding (NY: Oxford University Press, 2009), pp. 575-598.

[23] See for example Ben S. Bernanke, Speech at Harvard University, June 4, 2008.

[24] Claudia Goldin and Lawrence F. Katz, The Race Between Education and Technology: the Evolution of U.S. Educational Wage Differentials, 1890 to 2005, NBER, Working Paper 12984, Cambridge, MA, March 2007.

[25] David Autor, Frank Levy, and Richard Murnane, "The Skill Content of Recent Technological Change: An Empirical Exploration," Quarterly Journal of Economics, vol. 118, no. 5, November 2003, pp. 1279-1333.

[26] David H. Autor, Lawrence F. Katz, and Melissa S. Kearney, "Trends in Wage Inequality: Revising the Revisionists," Review of Economics and Statistics, vol. 90, no. 2 (May 2008), pp. 300-323.

[27] David Card and John E. DiNardo, "Skill-Biased Technological Change and Rising Wage Inequality: Some Problems and Puzzles," Journal of Labor Economics, vol. 20 (October 2002), pp. 733-783.

[28] Frank Levy and Peter Temin, Inequality and Institutions in 20th Century America, NBER, Working Paper 13106, Cambridge, MA, May 2007.

[29] Gary Burtless, "Demographic Transformation and Economic Inequality," in The Oxford Handbook of Economic Inequality, ed. Wiemer Salverda, Brian Nolan, and Timothy M. Smeeding (NY: Oxford University Press, 2009), pp. 435-454.

[30] The LIS and OECD use as their common measure disposable household money income. Disposable household income starts with market income, which includes earned income from wages, salaries, and self-employment as well as other cash income from private sources (e.g., property, private pensions, and child support). Public transfer payments (e.g., for old-age, sickness and disability, maternity and family support, unemployment, housing, and food) are added to market income. From this estimate of gross income, personal income tax and workers' social security contributions are subtracted to arrive at disposable cash income. This after-tax after-transfer income is then adjusted for household size.

[31] Anthony B. Atkinson, Lee Rainwater, and Timothy M. Smeeding, Income Distribution in OECD Countries: Evidence From the Luxembourg Income Study, OECD, 1995; Timothy Smeeding, Changing Income Inequality in OECD Countries: Updated Results from the Luxembourg Income Study, LIS, Working Paper 252, March 2000; Timothy M. Smeeding, Public Policy and Economic Inequality: The United States in Comparative Perspective, LIS, Working Paper 367, February 2004; and Andrea Brandolini and Timothy M. Smeeding, "Patterns of Economic Inequality in Western Democracies: Some Facts on Levels and Trends," Political Science and Politics, vol. 39, no. 1 (2006), pp. 21-26.

[32] As much as data availability allow, the countries presented in Table 3 are the same as those in Table 2. Differences tend to be very small between Gini coefficients by country for comparable time periods estimated from either the OECD or LIS databases.

[33] OECD, Divided We Stand: Why Inequality Keeps Rising, December 2011, 388 pp.

[34] Timothy M. Smeeding, "U.S. Income Inequality in a Cross-National Perspective: Why Are We So Different?," in James A. Auerbach and Richard S. Belous (ed), The Inequality Paradox: Growth of Income Disparity, National Policy Association, Washington, D.C., 2008.

[35] OECD, Growing Unequal? Income Distribution and Poverty in OECD Countries, October 2008.

[36] Chen Wang and Koen Caminada, Disentangling Income Inequality and the Redistributive Effect of Social Transfers and Taxes in 36 LIS Countries, LIS, Working Paper 567, July 2011, p. 14.

[37] Ibid., p. 27.

[38] Jonathan Heathcote, Fabrizio Perri, and Giovanni L. Violante, Unequal We Stand: An Empirical Analysis of Economic Inequality in the United States, 1967-2006, Federal Reserve Bank of Minneapolis, Research Department Staff Report 436, October 2009.

[39] Jason DeBacker, Bradley Heim, and Vasia Panousi, et al., Rising Inequality: Transitory or Permanent? New Evidence from a U.S. Panel of Household Income 1987-2006, Federal Reserve Board, Finance and Economics Discussion Series, Working Paper 2011-60, December 15, 2011. The authors note (pp. 26-27) that the finding may appear surprising because of "reductions in marginal tax rates, especially at the high end of the income distribution, in 2001 and 2003. However, such changes in top marginal tax rates were accompanied by (smaller) reductions in marginal tax rates for other income groups as well as significant expansions of the earned income tax credit and the child tax credit."

[40] Irwin Garfinkel, Lee Rainwater, and Timothy Smeeding, "A Re-examination of Welfare States and Inequality in Rich Nations: How In-kind Transfers and Indirect Taxes Change the Story," Journal of Policy Analysis and Management, vol. 25, no. 4 (2006), pp. 897-919.

[41] Gottschalk and Smeeding, "Cross-National Comparisons of Earnings and Income Inequality," Journal of Economic Literature, vol. 31, no. 2 (June 1997), pp. 633-687.

[42] Winfried Koeniger, Marco Leonardi, and Luca Nunziata, "Labor Market Institutions and Wage Inequality," Industrial and Labor Relations Review, vol. 60, no. 3 (April 2007), pp. 340-356.

[43] Daron Acemoglu, "Cross-Country Inequality Trends," The Economic Journal, vol. 113, no. 485 (February 2003), pp. F121-F149.

[44] Alberto Alesina, Rafael Di Tella, and Robert MacCulloch, "Inequality and Happiness: Are Europeans and Americans Different?," Journal of Public Economics, vol. 88 (2004), pp. 2009-2042.

[45] Isabel V. Sawhill, "Trends in Intergenerational Mobility," in Getting Ahead or Losing Ground: Economic Mobility in America, ed. Julia B. Isaacs, Isabel V. Sawhill, and Ron Haskins (Washington, DC: The Brookings Institution, 2008), 112 pp.

[46] Chul-In Lee and Gary Solon, "Trends in Intergenerational Income Mobility," Review of Economics and Statistics, vol. 91 (2009), pp. 766-772.

[47] Tom Hertz, "Trends in the Intergenerational Elasticity of Family Income in the United States," Industrial Relations, vol. 46, no. 1 (January 2007), pp. 22-50.

[48] Levine and Mazumder acknowledge that the correlation captures more than family background (e.g., neighborhood influence), but estimate that a large majority of the correlation may result from parent income.

[49] David I. Levine and Bhashkar Mazumder, "The Growing Importance of Family: Evidence from Brothers' Earnings," Industrial Relations, vol. 46, no. 1 (January 2007), p. 7-21.

[50] They created "synthetic families" by linking children's birth year and residence to the average income of parents in the same state in an earlier decennial census.

[51] Daniel Aaronson and Bhashkar Mazumder, "Intergenerational Economic Mobility in the United States, 1940 to 2000," Journal of Human Resources, vol. 43, no. 1 (2008), pp. 139-172.

[52] Bhashkar Mazumder, Is Intergenerational Economic Mobility Lower Now than in the Past?, The Federal Reserve Bank of Chicago, Essays on Issues, Number 297, April 2012, p. 3.

[53] Miles Corak, Do Poor Children Become Poor Adults? Lessons from a Cross Country Comparison of Generational Earnings Mobility, Institute for the Study of Labor (IZA), IZA Discussion Paper 1993, Bonn, Germany, March 2006.

[54] Maria Cervini-Pla, Intergenerational Earnings and Income Mobility in Spain, Munich Personal RePEc Archive, MPRA Paper No. 34942, November 2011, p. 21, http://mpra.ub.uni-muenchen.de/34942.

[55] Patrizio Piranio, "Comparable Estimates of Intergenerational Income Mobility in Italy," The B.E. Journal of Economic Analysis & Policy, vol. 7, no. 2 (2007), p. 11.

[56] Markus Jantti, Knut Roed, and Robin Naylor et al., American Exceptionalism in a New Light: A Comparison of Intergenerational Earnings Mobility in the Nordic Countries, the United Kingdom and the United States, Institute for the Study of Labor (IZA), IZA Discussion Paper 1938, Bonn, Germany, January 2006, p. 28.

[57] Economic Mobility Project, Pursuing the American Dream: Economic Mobility Across Generations, The Pew Charitable Trusts, July 2012.

[58] Katharine Bradbury, Trends in U.S. Family Income Mobility, 1969-2006, Federal Reserve Bank of Boston, Working Paper 11-10, October 20, 2011, p. 27.

[59] Gregory Acs and Seth Zimmerman, U.S. Intragenerational Economic Mobility from 1984 to 2004: Trends and Implications, The Pew Charitable Trusts, Economic Mobility Project, October 2008, p. 12.

[60] Gerald Auten and Geoffrey Gee, "Income Mobility in the United States: New Evidence from Income Tax Data," National Tax Journal, vol. LXII, no. 2 (June 2009), p. 313.

[61] Diaz-Gimenez et al., Distributions of Earnings, Income, and Wealth.

[62] Richard V. Burkhauser and Kenneth A. Couch, "Intragenerational Inequality and Intertemporal Mobility," in The Oxford Handbook of Economic Inequality, ed. Wiemer Salverda, Brian Nolan and Timothy M. Smeeding (New York: Oxford University Press, 2009), pp. 522-545.

In: Income Distribution in the United States ISBN: 978-1-63482-675-4
Editor: Clayton Diaz

Chapter 4

The Distribution of Household Income and Federal Taxes, 2011*

Kevin Perese

Notes and Definitions

Numbers in the text, tables, and figures may not add up to totals because of rounding. Dollar amounts are generally rounded to the nearest hundred.

Unless otherwise indicated, all years referred to in this report are calendar years.

Market income consists of labor income, business income, capital gains (profits realized from the sale of assets), capital income excluding capital gains, income received in retirement for past services, and other sources of income.

Government transfers are cash payments and in-kind benefits from social insurance and other government assistance programs. Those transfers include payments and benefits from federal, state, and local governments.

Before-tax income is market income plus government transfers.

Federal taxes include individual income taxes, payroll (or social insurance) taxes, corporate income taxes, and excise taxes. In this analysis, those taxes for a given year are the amount a household owes on the basis of

---

* This is an edited, reformatted and augmented version of a report issued by the Congressional Budget Office, November 2014.

income received in that year, regardless of when the taxes are paid. Taxes from those four sources accounted for approximately 92 percent of federal revenues in fiscal year 2011. Revenue sources not examined in this report include states' deposits for unemployment insurance, estate and gift taxes, customs duties, and miscellaneous receipts.

After-tax income is before-tax income minus federal taxes.

Average federal tax rates are calculated by dividing federal taxes by before-tax income.

Income groups are created by ranking households by their size-adjusted income. Specifically, income is adjusted for differences in household size by dividing income by the square root of the number of people in the household. A household consists of people sharing a housing unit, regardless of their relationships. Each income quintile (fifth) contains approximately equal numbers of people but different numbers of households. Similarly, each percentile (hundredth) contains approximately equal numbers of people but different numbers of households. If a household has negative income (that is, if its business or investment losses are larger than its other income), it is excluded from the lowest income group but included in totals.

When examining household income over time, income is adjusted for inflation using the personal consumption expenditures price index, which is calculated by the Bureau of Economic Analysis.

Some of the figures have shaded vertical bars that indicate the duration of recessions. (A recession extends from the peak of a business cycle to its trough.)

Supplemental data showing household income and average federal tax rates for households with children, elderly childless households, and nonelderly childless households are posted along with this report on CBO's website (www.cbo.gov/publication/49440).

SUMMARY

In 2011, according to the Congressional Budget Office's (CBO's) estimates, average household market income— a comprehensive income measure that consists of labor income, business income, capital income (including capital gains), and retirement income—was approximately $81,000. Government transfers, which include benefits from programs such as Social Security, Medicare, and unemployment insurance, averaged approximately $13,000 per household. The sum of those two amounts, which equals before-tax income, was about $94,000, on average. Federal taxes as examined in this report comprise four separate sources: individual income taxes, payroll (or social insurance) taxes, corporate income taxes, and excise taxes. Taken together, those taxes were about $17,000 per household, on average, in 2011. Thus, average household income after taxes was about $77,000, and the average federal tax rate (federal taxes divided by before-tax income) was 17.6 percent.

How Were Income and Federal Taxes Distributed in 2011?

Before-tax income was unevenly distributed across households in 2011. Average before-tax income among households in the lowest one-fifth (or quintile) of the distribution of before-tax income was approximately $25,000 in 2011, CBO estimates (see Table 1). Among households in the middle income quintile, average before-tax income was about $66,000. Relative to those two income groups, households in the highest income quintile had average before-tax income that was much higher—approximately $246,000.

Overall, federal taxes are progressive, meaning that average tax rates generally rise as income increases. Households in the lowest income quintile paid about $500 in federal taxes in 2011, on average, which amounted to an average federal tax rate of about 2 percent, CBO estimates.[1] Households in the middle quintile paid about $7,000 in federal taxes, and households in the highest quintile paid about $58,000 in federal taxes, which results in average federal tax rates of approximately 11 percent and 23 percent, respectively.

As a result of the progressive federal tax structure, households in the highest quintile of before-tax income paid a greater share of federal taxes in 2011 than they received in before-tax income, while households in each of the other quintiles paid a smaller share of federal taxes than they received in before-tax income (see Figure 1). Households in the highest income quintile received a little more than half of total before-tax income and paid more than two-thirds of all federal taxes in 2011. In contrast, households in the lowest income quintile received approximately 5 percent of total before-tax income in 2011 and paid less than 1 percent of all federal taxes, CBO estimates.

The progressive federal tax structure also results in a distribution of after-tax income that is slightly more even than that of before-tax income. Households in the lowest income quintile received approximately 6 percent of after-tax income in 2011, compared with 5 percent of before-tax income, and households in the highest income quintile received about 48 percent of after-tax income, compared with 52 percent of before-tax income, CBO estimates.

How Did Changes in Tax Rules Between 2011 and 2013 Affect Average Federal Tax Rates?

Tax rules have changed since 2011 in several important ways. Most notably, by 2013, several provisions affecting high-income taxpayers—originally enacted in 2001 (in the Economic Growth and Tax Relief Reconciliation Act, or EGTRRA) and 2003 (in the Jobs and Growth Tax Relief Reconciliation Act, or JGTRRA)—were allowed to expire.

Table 1. Average Household Income, Transfers, and Taxes, by before-Tax Income Group, 2011

Dollars	Lowest Quintile	Second Quintile	Middle Quintile	Fourth Quintile	Highest Quintile	All Households
Market Income	15,500	29,600	49,800	83,300	234,700	80,600
Government Transfers	9,100	15,700	16,500	14,100	11,000	13,300
Before-Tax Income	24,600	45,300	66,400	97,500	245,700	93,900
Federal Taxes	500	3,200	7,400	14,800	57,500	16,600
After-Tax Income	24,100	42,100	59,000	82,600	188,200	77,300

Source: Congressional Budget Office.

Notes: Market income consists of labor income, business income, capital gains (profits realized from the sale of assets), capital income excluding capital gains, income received in retirement for past services, and other sources of income.

Government transfers are cash payments and in-kind benefits from social insurance and other government assistance programs. Those transfers include payments and benefits from federal, state, and local governments.

Before-tax income is market income plus government transfers.

Federal taxes include individual income taxes, payroll taxes, corporate income taxes, and excise taxes. After-tax income is before-tax income minus federal taxes.

Income groups are created by ranking households by before-tax income, adjusted for household size. Quintiles (fifths) contain equal numbers of people.

For more detailed definitions of income, see the appendix.

In addition, payroll tax rates that had been reduced in 2011 and 2012 were reset to their previous, higher levels in 2013, and new taxes for high-income taxpayers enacted in the Affordable Care Act took effect in 2013.[2] As part of this analysis, CBO estimated the effects of those changes on the distribution of federal taxes.[3]

If the income distribution was unchanged between 2011 and 2013, the average federal tax rate for all households would have been 1.7 percentage points higher under 2013 tax rules than it was in 2011, CBO estimates. Although average federal tax rates would have increased by about 1 percentage point across much of the income distribution, the average tax rate for households in the top 1 percent of the income distribution would have increased by an estimated 4.3 percentage points.

What Are the Trends in the Distribution of Household Income and Federal Taxes?

Over the 33-year period from 1979 to 2011, average after-tax income—which equals market income plus government transfers minus federal taxes—grew at significantly different rates at different points in the income scale.[4] For households in the top 1 percent of the income distribution, inflation-adjusted after-tax income grew at an estimated average rate of 3.5 percent per year. As a result, inflation-adjusted after-tax income was 200 percent higher in 2011 than it was in 1979 for households in that group. In contrast, households in the bottom quintile experienced inflation-adjusted after-tax income growth of 1.2 percent per year, on average. Consequently, inflation-adjusted after-tax income was 48 percent higher in 2011 than it was in 1979 for that income group. Those differences in growth rates for after-tax income are largely attributable to differences in growth rates for market income, although changes in taxes and transfers played a role as well.[5]

Average federal tax rates fluctuate over time because of changes in tax law and changes in the composition and distribution of income. In 2011, average federal tax rates were near their lowest levels since 1979 for households in most of the income groups examined in this report. The only exception was for households in the top 1 percent of the income distribution. For that group, the average federal tax rate in 2011 was near its lowest level since the early 1990s (see Figure 2).

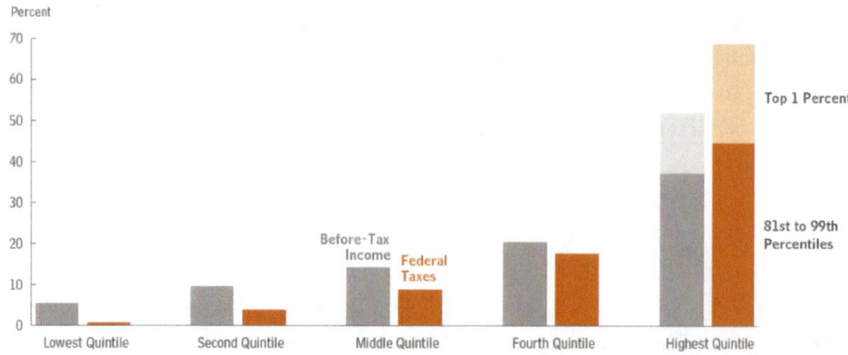

Source: Congressional Budget Office.

Notes: Before-tax income is market income plus government transfers. Market income consists of labor income, business income, capital gains (profits realized from the sale of assets), capital income excluding capital gains, income received in retirement for past services, and other sources of income. Government transfers are cash payments and in-kind benefits from social insurance and other government assistance programs. Those transfers include payments and benefits from federal, state, and local governments.

Federal taxes include individual income taxes, payroll taxes, corporate income taxes, and excise taxes.

Income groups are created by ranking households by before-tax income, adjusted for household size. Quintiles (fifths) contain equal numbers of people; percentiles (hundredths) contain equal numbers of people as well.

For more detailed definitions of income, see the appendix.

Figure 1. Shares of Before-Tax Income and Federal Taxes, by Before-Tax Income Group, 2011.

CBO estimates that average federal tax rates under 2013 law would be higher—relative to tax rates in 2011— across the income spectrum. The estimated rates under 2013 law would still be well below the average rates from 1979 through 2011 for the bottom four income quintiles, slightly below the average rate over that period for households in the 81st through 99th percentiles, and well above the average rate over that period for households in the top 1 percent of the income distribution.

Government transfers and federal taxes lessen income inequality because federal taxes are progressive and payments from government transfer programs generally decline as a share of income as income rises. Between 1979 and 2011, government transfers reduced income inequality to a greater extent than federal taxes, based on a standard measure of inequality known as the Gini index. In 2011, government transfers accounted for approximately two-thirds of the reduction in income inequality observed between market income and after-tax income.

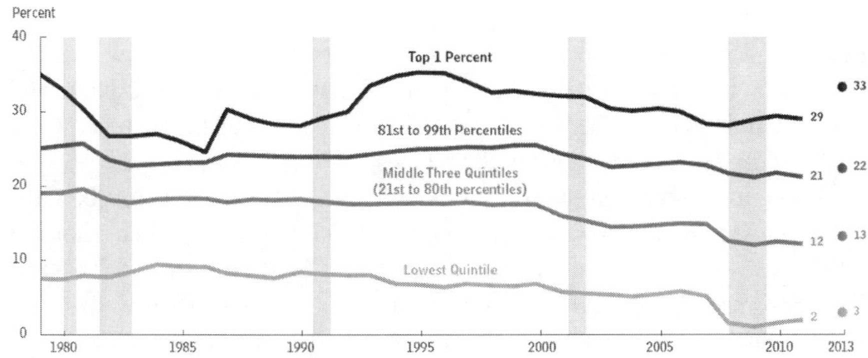

Source: Congressional Budget Office.

Notes: Average federal tax rates are calculated by dividing federal taxes by before-tax income.

Before-tax income is market income plus government transfers. Market income consists of labor income, business income, capital gains (profits realized from the sale of assets), capital income excluding capital gains, income received in retirement for past services, and other sources of income. Government transfers are cash payments and in-kind benefits from social insurance and other government assistance programs. Those transfers include payments and benefits from federal, state, and local governments.

Federal taxes include individual income taxes, payroll taxes, corporate income taxes, and excise taxes.

Federal tax rates for 2013 are calculated by applying individual income tax and payroll tax rules in place in 2013 to the income distribution observed in 2011.

Income groups are created by ranking households by before-tax income, adjusted for household size. Quintiles (fifths) contain equal numbers of people; percentiles (hundredths) contain equal numbers of people as well.

For more detailed definitions of income, see the appendix.

Figure 2. Average Federal Tax Rates, by Before-Tax Income Group, 1979 to 2011 and Projected Under 2013 Law.

INCOME AND TAXES ACROSS HOUSEHOLDS IN 2011

Throughout this report, CBO analyzes the distribution of three separate measures of income. The first, market income, is broadly measured. It equals the sum of labor income, business income, capital income (including capital gains), and retirement income. Labor income includes cash wages and salaries, including amounts allocated by employees to 401(k) plans; employer-paid health insurance premiums; the employer's share of payroll taxes for Social Security, Medicare, and federal unemployment insurance; and the share of corporate income taxes borne by workers (see Box 1).[6] The second measure examined in this report is before-tax income, which equals market income plus government transfers.[7] The third measure examined is after-tax income, which equals before-tax income minus federal taxes.[8]

Average market income for households in 2011 was $80,600, CBO estimates.[9] On average, households received $13,300 in government transfers in that year— $9,100 from Social Security and Medicare and $4,200 from other government transfers. Before-tax income, on average, was therefore $93,900. In 2011, households paid an estimated $16,600 in federal taxes, resulting in average household after-tax income of $77,300. The average federal tax rate in 2011 (which is equal to federal tax liabilities divided by before-tax income)—17.6 percent—was the sum of four average tax rates: individual income taxes (8.4 percent), payroll taxes (6.7 percent), corporate income taxes (1.9 percent), and excise taxes (0.7 percent).

All of those measures—market income, government transfers, before-tax income, federal tax rates, and after-tax income—vary across the income scale, sometimes significantly. Market income is highly skewed toward the top of the income distribution: Households in the top quintile of the distribution of market income in 2011 received an estimated 58.1 percent of total market income, while households in the bottom quintile received an estimated 2.2 percent. Because government transfers constitute a larger share of market income toward the bottom of the income distribution, before-tax income is somewhat more evenly distributed across the income scale than market income—but it is still very skewed toward the top of the distribution. The progressivity of the federal tax system reduces the level of income inequality further by disproportionately decreasing income at the top of the distribution. After-tax income, therefore, is more equally distributed across the income scale than before-tax income. Nonetheless, households in the top quintile of the distribution of before-tax income in 2011 received an estimated 48.2 percent of total after-tax income, while households in the bottom quintile received an estimated 6.3 percent.

Market Income Across the Income Scale

Market income is highly skewed toward households at the top of the income distribution (see Figure 3). In 2011, households in the lowest quintile of market income earned an estimated 2.2 percent of total market income, or about $7,900 per household, on average.[10] Households in the middle quintile earned 13.0 percent of total market income (or about $55,400, on average), and households in the top quintile earned 58.1 percent (or about $240,800, on average). Within the top quintile of households, market income is also skewed toward the very top of the income distribution. The approximately 1.1 million households in the top 1 percent of the market income distribution earned 16.9 percent of total market income, or about $1.4 million per household, on average.

In 2011, labor income made up the largest share—at least two-thirds—of market income for each income quintile (see Table 2). However, the share of market income derived from labor falls off significantly for households in the top 1 percent of the distribution (although the dollar amount continues to increase). Labor income accounts for an estimated 73 percent of market income among households in the 96th through 99th percentiles but only 37 percent of market income among households in the top 1 percent. Capital income (including realized capital gains) increases significantly for the top 1 percent of households and therefore makes up a much larger proportion of market income, pushing down the share attributable to labor.

Box 1. Issues with Measuring Income

In its broadest—but most difficult to measure— form, income can be viewed as the value of all goods and services consumed plus any net change in the purchasing power of wealth over a given period. In its analyses of the distribution of income and taxes, the Congressional Budget Office (CBO) strives to measure income as broadly as possible and thus includes in income some items that people may not usually consider to be part of income. For example, CBO counts taxes paid by businesses as part of household before-tax income; because those taxes are ultimately borne by households in the form of reduced income, CBO adds them to before-tax income in order to measure more accurately what a household's ability to consume would have been in the absence of those taxes.

Similarly, CBO includes in households' before-tax income employers' contributions to health insurance and the cost of government health insurance programs such as Medicare and Medicaid. Although not provided in cash, those items are included in income because they increase people's ability to consume goods and services.

However, the measure of income used by CBO departs in significant ways from a theoretically ideal measure. Many of those departures occur because of limitations in the underlying source data from which CBO constructs its estimates.[1] As a result, CBO's estimates of the distribution of income might differ considerably from the distribution of income measured in a more ideal way. The direction and size of any such differences—and how they have changed over time—are uncertain. The following discussion focuses on six notable ways in which CBO's measure of income differs from a theoretically ideal measure.

Unrealized Capital Gains

An increase in the value of an asset represents income to the owner of that asset, regardless of whether the asset is sold. The tax system, however, records that income and levies tax on it only when the owner sells the asset and realizes the gain, in large part because of the difficulty of measuring increases in the value of assets as they accrue if they are not sold. CBO follows the treatment of the tax system and includes realized capital gains in income; accrued but unrealized gains are excluded.

Effects of Inflation on Capital Income

An ideal measure of income would include only the portions of interest income and realized capital gains that reflect increases in people's ability to consume goods and services; it would not include the portions of interest income and capital gains that reflect changes in the prices of goods and services because those portions do not correspond to increases in purchasing power. Tax data and survey data, however, do not contain the information necessary to accurately remove the parts of income from those sources that reflect changes in prices over the relevant periods. Therefore, CBO counts nominal income from interest and realized capital gains in its measure of before-tax income without any adjustment for the amounts attributable to inflation.

Retirement Income

In an ideal measure of income, income from defined benefit pension plans, defined contribution pension plans, and individual retirement accounts would be counted when the benefits from those plans accrued. However, survey data and administrative data do not capture well the increases in assets in individual households' retirement accounts or in the value of benefits promised under defined benefit plans. Consequently, CBO measures retirement income when it is withdrawn from households' accounts or received as benefits.

Business Income

The organizational structure of a business determines when profits from that business need to be distributed to its shareholders. Businesses with certain structures, such as partnerships and S corporations, must annually distribute all profits to their shareholders, who are required to report those profits as income through the individual income tax system. Businesses with other structures, such as C corporations, may choose to retain their profits rather than distribute them as dividends. An ideal measure of income would include all income derived from businesses' profits in a given period, regardless of whether those profits were distributed or retained.

However, CBO includes in its income measure only profits that are distributed; profits that are retained by C corporations are not included, although some are captured in subsequent dividend payments or realized capital gains.

Imputed Income From Owner-Occupied Housing

Landlords receive rental payments for the property they own, and those payments are generally included in their reported income. By contrast, the value of housing services received by homeowners from the property they own is not included in their reported income. An ideal measure of income would include that value (net of depreciation, interest payments, and taxes), but because the necessary data are not available, CBO does not impute the value of the services derived from owner-occupied housing.

Similarly, CBO does not include the implicit income from other durable goods, such as automobiles, in its measure of household income.

Misreporting of Income

The Statistics of Income data used in this report are the most comprehensive and highest quality data about incomes that are available, but some income is misreported in those data because of tax avoidance. CBO also uses information from survey data in its calculation of household income (particularly for transfer payments and other nontaxable sources of income), and that information is less reliable because it relies on respondents' recall of their past income. As a result of those problems, total income reported in tax and survey data taken together is less than total income in the economy. How that discrepancy is distributed across the income scale, however, is uncertain, and CBO makes no attempt to correct for any distributional effects of the underreporting of income.

[1] The measures of income used by CBO for its analyses of the distribution of income and taxes are constructed from data on individual income tax returns prepared by the Statistics of Income division of the Internal Revenue Service and from household survey data collected by the Census Bureau. See the appendix for more details.

Before-Tax Income across the Income Scale

Market income is by far the largest component of before-tax income for all income groups—ranging from an estimated 63 percent of before-tax income for households in the lowest quintile of before-tax income to about 99 percent of before-tax income for households in the top 1 percent (see Table 3).

Government transfers increase income across the entire income distribution, on average, but make up a significantly larger share of before-tax income for lower-income groups than for higher-income groups.[11] In 2011, government transfers accounted for more than one-third of before-tax income for households in the lowest and second-lowest income quintiles and one-quarter of before-tax income for households in the middle quintile, CBO estimates. Those shares fall off significantly for higher-income households. Among households in the highest income quintile, less than 5 percent of their before-tax income comes from transfers; for households in the top 1 percent, that figure is less than 1 percent.

Social Security and Medicare are the two largest government transfer programs. Transfers from those programs are provided mostly to elderly households, many of which have low market income. Other transfers—including payments from the Supplemental Nutrition Assistance Program and benefits from Medicaid and the Children's Health Insurance Program—are provided even more disproportionately to households in the lower portion of the income distribution.

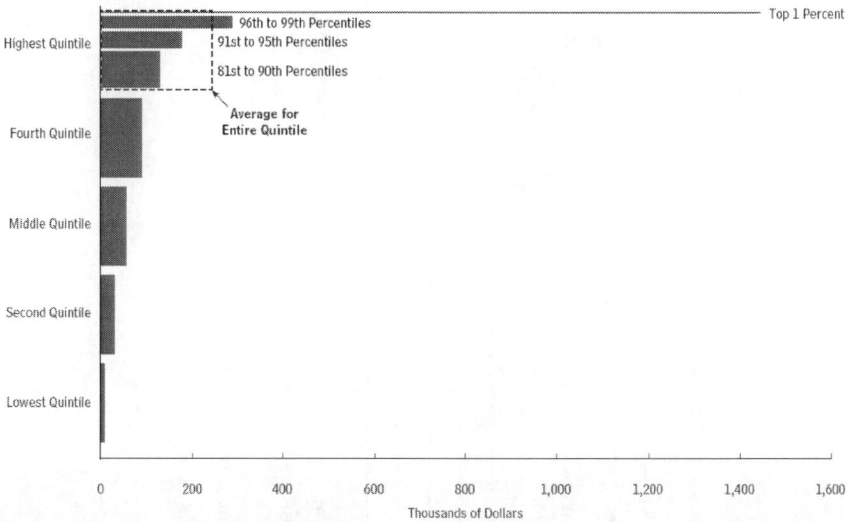

Source: Congressional Budget Office.

Notes: Market income consists of labor income, business income, capital gains (profits realized from the sale of assets), capital income excluding capital gains, income received in retirement for past services, and other sources of income.

Income groups are created by ranking households by market income, adjusted for household size. Quintiles (fifths) contain equal numbers of people; percentiles (hundredths) contain equal numbers of people as well.

For more detailed definitions of income, see the appendix.

Figure 3. Market Income, by Market Income Group, 2011.

Despite government transfers going predominantly to lower-income households, the fact that total transfers make up less than 15 percent of total before-tax income means that the distribution of before-tax income is only slightly less uneven than the distribution of market income.

Table 2. Components of Market Income, by Market Income Group, 2011

			Quintiles					Percentiles		
	Lowest	Second	Middle	Fourth	Highest	All Households	81st to 90th	91st to 95th	96th to 99th	Top 1
Market Income (Dollars)	7,900	31,100	55,400	89,600	240,800	80,600	132,400	180,900	293,000	1,447,500
Market Income (Percent)										
Labor income	67	75	80	83	67	74	83	81	73	37
Business income	11	4	3	3	11	7	3	5	11	22
Capital income and gains	5	4	3	3	15	10	4	5	10	36
Other income[a]	17	17	13	11	7	8	9	9	7	4

Source: Congressional Budget Office.

Notes: Income groups are created by ranking households by market income, adjusted for household size. Quintiles (fifths) contain equal numbers of people; percentiles (hundredths) contain equal numbers of people as well.

For more detailed definitions of income, see the appendix.

a. Includes income received in retirement for past services and other sources of income.

In 2011, households in the lowest quintile received an estimated 5.3 percent of total before-tax income, or about $24,600 per household, according to CBO's estimates (see Figure 1).[12] Households in the middle fifth received 14.1 percent of the total, or about $66,400 per household. Households in the top quintile received 51.9 percent of the total, or about $245,700 per household.

Before-tax income within the top quintile is also skewed toward the very top of the income distribution. Households in the 81st through 90th percentiles (the bottom half of the top quintile) received 14.6 percent of total before-tax income and had an average before-tax income of $138,800. Households in the top 1 percent of the income distribution also received 14.6 percent of total before-tax income, which amounted to $1.4 million per household, on average, CBO estimates.

Federal Taxes Across the Income Scale

Average federal tax rates generally rise with income.[13] In 2011, households in the bottom fifth of the distribution of before-tax income paid an estimated 1.9 percent of their before-tax income in federal taxes, households in the middle quintile paid 11.2 percent, and households in the top quintile paid 23.4 percent. Furthermore, average tax rates within the top quintile continued to increase as income rose, and households in the top 1 percent of the before-tax income distribution had an average tax rate of 29.0 percent (see Figure 4).

Because average federal tax rates are progressive, the share of taxes paid by higher-income households exceeds their share of before-tax income, and the opposite is true for lower-income households (see Figure 1). In 2011, households in the highest quintile received an estimated 51.9 percent of before-tax income and paid 68.7 percent of federal taxes; households in the top 1 percent received 14.6 percent of before-tax income and paid 24.0 percent of federal taxes. In all other quintiles, the share of federal taxes was smaller than the share of before-tax income: Households in the bottom quintile received 5.3 percent of income and paid 0.6 percent of taxes, and households in the middle quintile received 14.1 percent of income and paid 8.9 percent of taxes.

Table 3. Components of Before-Tax Income, by Before-Tax Income Group, 2011

			Quintiles					Percentiles		
	Lowest	Second	Middle	Fourth	Highest	All Households	81st to 90th	91st to 95th	96th to 99th	Top 1
Before-Tax Income (Dollars)	24,600	45,300	66,400	97,500	245,700	93,900	138,800	186,700	299,000	1,453,100
Before-Tax Income (Percent) Market income	63	65	75	86	96	86	91	94	97	99
Labor income	54	56	62	69	62	63	73	73	68	37
Business income	6	3	2	2	11	6	3	5	10	22
Capital income and gains	1	1	2	3	15	9	4	6	10	36
Other income	2	5	9	11	8	7	11	11	8	4
Government transfers	37	35	25	14	4	14	9	6	3	1
Social Security	9	12	11	7	2	6	4	3	2	*
Medicare	9	9	7	4	1	4	2	2	1	*
Medicaid	9	8	4	1	*	2	1	*	*	*
Other cash and in-kind	10	6	4	2	1	2	1	1	*	*

Source: Congressional Budget Office.

Notes: Before-tax income is market income plus government transfers.

Market income consists of labor income, business income, capital gains (profits realized from the sale of assets), capital income excluding capital gains, income received in retirement for past services, and other sources of income.

Government transfers are cash payments and in-kind benefits from social insurance and other government assistance programs. Those transfers include payments and benefits from federal, state, and local governments.

Income groups are created by ranking households by before-tax income, adjusted for household size. Quintiles (fifths) contain equal numbers of people; percentiles (hundredths) contain equal numbers of people as well.

For more detailed definitions of income, see the appendix. * = between zero and 0.5 percent.

Individual Income Taxes

Most of the progressivity of the federal tax system derives from the individual income tax. In 2011, households in the lowest quintile of before-tax income had an average tax rate for the individual income tax of -7.5 percent, and households in the second quintile had a rate of -1.3 percent, CBO estimates. (An income quintile has a negative average income tax rate if refundable tax credits in that quintile exceed other income tax liabilities.)[14] The average individual income tax rate was 2.4 percent for the middle quintile, 5.8 percent for the fourth quintile, and 14.2 percent for the top quintile (see Figure 5). Households in the top 1 percent of the income distribution paid 20.3 percent of their before-tax income in individual income taxes, on average.[15]

Payroll Taxes

Average rates for payroll taxes are very similar across most of the income distribution but lower at the top of the distribution. In 2011, the average payroll tax rate was 7.1 percent for households in the lowest quintile of before-tax income, 6.7 percent for the second quintile, 7.2 percent for the middle quintile, and 7.8 percent for the fourth quintile, CBO estimates. The rate for the highest income quintile was 5.9 percent. The average rate among households in the top percentile was significantly lower—2.1 percent—than the rates for all other households, in part because more of the earnings for those households were above the maximum earnings subject to Social Security payroll taxes ($106,800 in 2011) and in part because earnings were a smaller share of their total income. Payroll taxes account for more than half of total federal taxes among households in all but the top quintile, on average.

Corporate Income Taxes

The average corporate income tax borne by households increases with income. CBO allocates most of that tax in proportion to each household's share of total capital income (including adjusted capital gains), which constitutes a larger share of income at the top of the distribution.[16] In 2011, the average corporate income tax rate—corporate taxes divided by before-tax household income—was 2.9 percent for households in the highest quintile and between 0.6 percent and 0.9 percent for households in the other four income quintiles, CBO estimates. The share of the total corporate tax burden borne by households in the highest income quintile was 78.6 percent in 2011, and the share borne by households in the top 1 percent of the income distribution was 48.7 percent.

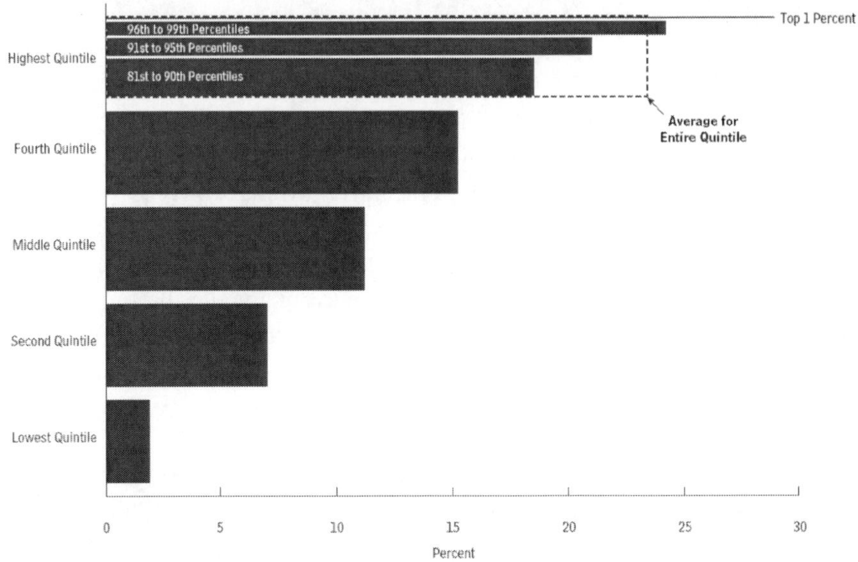

Source: Congressional Budget Office.

Notes: Average federal tax rates are calculated by dividing federal taxes by before-tax income.

Before-tax income is market income plus government transfers. Market income consists of labor income, business income, capital gains (profits realized from the sale of assets), capital income excluding capital gains, income received in retirement for past services, and other sources of income. Government transfers are cash payments and in-kind benefits from social insurance and other government assistance programs. Those transfers include payments and benefits from federal, state, and local governments.

Federal taxes include individual income taxes, payroll taxes, corporate income taxes, and excise taxes.

Income groups are created by ranking households by before-tax income, adjusted for household size. Quintiles (fifths) contain equal numbers of people; percentiles (hundredths) contain equal numbers of people as well.

For more detailed definitions of income, see the appendix.

Figure 4. Average Federal Tax Rates, by Before-Tax Income Group, 2011.

Excise Taxes

Sales of a wide variety of goods and services are subject to federal excise taxes. Most of the revenues raised come from taxes on the sale of motor fuels (gasoline and diesel fuel), tobacco products, alcoholic beverages, and aviation-related goods and services (such as aviation fuel and airline tickets). The burden of excise taxes relative to income is greatest for lower-income households, which tend to spend a larger share of their income on those taxed goods and services. In 2011, average excise tax rates were 1.6 percent for households in the lowest income quintile, 0.9 percent for households in the middle income quintile, and 0.4 percent for households in the highest income quintile, CBO estimates.

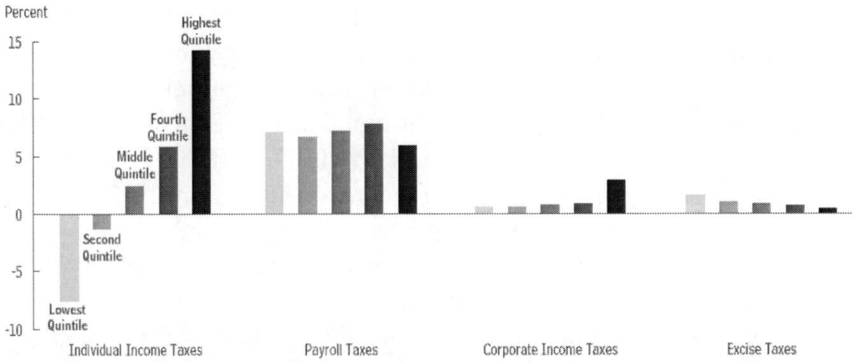

Source: Congressional Budget Office.

Notes: Average federal tax rates are calculated by dividing federal taxes by before-tax income.

Before-tax income is market income plus government transfers. Market income consists of labor income, business income, capital gains (profits realized from the sale of assets), capital income excluding capital gains, income received in retirement for past services, and other sources of income. Government transfers are cash payments and in-kind benefits from social insurance and other government assistance programs. Those transfers include payments and benefits from federal, state, and local governments.

Negative average tax rates for individual income taxes result when refundable tax credits, such as the earned income tax credit and the child tax credit, exceed the other income tax liabilities of the households in an income group.

Income groups are created by ranking households by before-tax income, adjusted for household size. Quintiles (fifths) contain equal numbers of people.

For more detailed definitions of income, see the appendix.

Figure 5. Average Federal Tax Rates, by Before-Tax Income Group and Tax Source, 2011.

After-Tax Income Across the Income Scale

For each income group in 2011, the average household paid a positive amount of federal taxes, so average after-tax income was lower than average before-tax income. Because average federal tax rates rise with income, the difference between before-tax and after-tax income grows as income rises and the distribution of after-tax income is slightly more even than the distribution of before-tax income. In the lowest quintile of before-tax income, average after-tax income was approximately $500 lower than average before-tax income ($24,600 versus $24,100); for households in the middle quintile of before-tax income, the difference was approximately $7,400 ($66,400 versus $59,000); for households in the highest quintile of before-tax income, the difference was approximately $57,500 ($245,700 versus $188,200); see Table 1. For households in the top 1 percent, the difference was approximately $421,000 ($1,453,000 versus $1,032,000), CBO estimates.

Another metric used to examine how the distributions of after-tax income and before-tax income differ is the differences in the shares of those income measures going to each income group (see Figure 6). According to CBO's estimates, households in the bottom four quintiles of the distribution of before-tax income received shares of after-tax income that were roughly 1 percentage point larger than their shares of before-tax income (the exact amounts were 1.0, 1.3, 1.1, and 0.6 percentage points from the first quintile to the fourth quintile, respectively).

In contrast, for households in the top quintile, the share of after-tax income was 3.7 percentage points lower than the share of before-tax income (48.2 percent of after-tax income versus 51.9 percent of before-tax income). More than half of that difference for the top income quintile— 2 percentage points—was attributable to the difference between the shares of after-tax and before-tax income for the top 1 percent of the income distribution. Households in that income group received about 14.6 percent of before-tax income and 12.6 percent of after-tax income.

After-tax income also reflects the impact of government transfers on the distribution of income. The distributional effects of the combination of government transfers and federal taxes can be seen by examining differences in the distributions of market income (income before government transfers and federal taxes) and after-tax income (see Figure 7).[17] Those differences were most significant for households in the lowest and highest quintiles of market income. Households in the lowest income quintile had a share of after-tax income that was 7.2 percentage points higher than their share of market income— 9.4 percent versus 2.2 percent. In contrast, households in the highest income quintile had a share of after-tax income that was 10.8 percentage points lower than their share of market income—47.3 percent versus 58.1 percent.

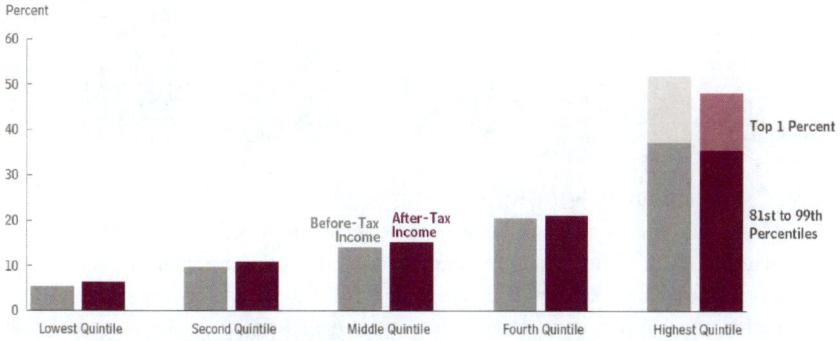

Source: Congressional Budget Office.

Notes: Before-tax income is market income plus government transfers. Market income consists of labor income, business income, capital gains (profits realized from the sale of assets), capital income (excluding capital gains), income received in retirement for past services, and other sources of income. Government transfers are cash payments and in-kind benefits from social insurance and other government assistance programs. Those transfers include payments and benefits from federal, state, and local governments.

After-tax income is before-tax income minus federal taxes. Federal taxes include individual income taxes, payroll taxes, corporate income taxes, and excise taxes.

Income groups are created by ranking households by before-tax income, adjusted for household size. Quintiles (fifths) contain equal numbers of people; percentiles (hundredths) contain equal numbers of people as well.

For more detailed definitions of income, see the appendix.

Figure 6. Shares of Before-Tax and After-Tax Income, by Before-Tax Income Group, 2011.

The differences in the shares of market income and after-tax income were not as large for households in the other three quintiles. Households in the second and middle quintiles had larger shares of after-tax income than market income, whereas households in the fourth quintile had a smaller share of after-tax income than market income.

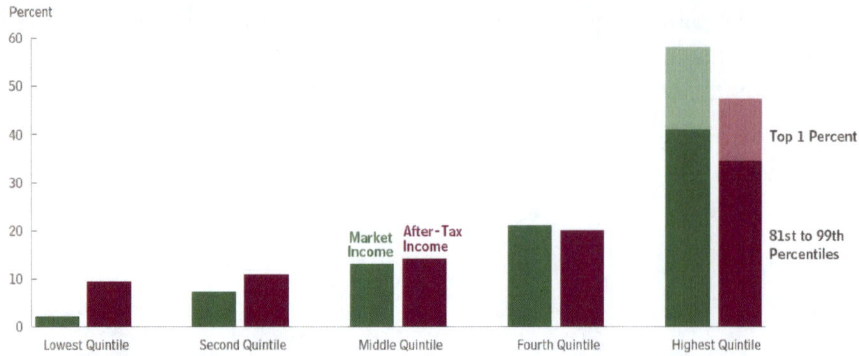

Source: Congressional Budget Office.

Notes: Market income consists of labor income, business income, capital gains (profits realized from the sale of assets), capital income excluding capital gains, income received in retirement for past services, and other sources of income.

After-tax income is market income plus government transfers minus federal taxes. Government transfers are cash payments and in-kind benefits from social insurance and other government assistance programs. Those transfers include payments and benefits from federal, state, and local governments. Federal taxes include individual income taxes, payroll taxes, corporate income taxes, and excise taxes.

Income groups are created by ranking households by market income, adjusted for household size. Quintiles (fifths) contain equal numbers of people; percentiles (hundredths) contain equal numbers of people as well.

For more detailed definitions of income, see the appendix.

Figure 7. Shares of Market and After-Tax Income, by Market Income Group, 2011.

FEDERAL TAXES UNDER 2013 TAX RULES

Between 2011 and 2013, tax rules changed significantly—and probably shifted the distribution of federal taxes in notable ways. CBO estimated the effects of major changes to individual income tax and payroll tax provisions that occurred between 2011 and 2013 by simulating tax liabilities under 2013 tax rules using reported 2011 incomes.[18] Those estimates do not include any shifts in the income distribution that have occurred between 2011 and 2013 attributable to either the continued recovery of the economy since the last recession or any behavioral effects in response to the tax law changes.

Changes in Tax Rules between 2011 and 2013

The three most significant changes in provisions of the individual income tax and payroll tax between 2011 and 2013 were the following:

- Several income tax provisions affecting high-income taxpayers, originally enacted in EGTRRA and JGTRRA, expired at the end of 2012;
- Payroll tax rates that had been reduced in 2011 and 2012 were reset to their previous, higher levels in 2013; and
- New taxes for high-income taxpayers enacted in the Affordable Care Act took effect in 2013.

Although the tax rules enacted in EGTRRA and JGTRRA were originally scheduled to expire at the end of 2010, they were extended through 2012 by the Tax Relief, Unemployment Insurance Reauthorization, and Job Creation Act of 2010. Therefore, the tax rules in effect in 2011 reflected the changes made in EGTRRA and JGTRRA, which lowered tax rates on ordinary income (by creating a 10 percent bracket and expanding the 15 percent bracket) and on capital gains realizations and dividends and enlarged the standard deduction for married couples and the child tax credit. The 2010 tax law also extended for two years most of the tax credits enacted in the American Recovery and Reinvestment Act of 2009 (ARRA), although the Making Work Pay tax credit was allowed to expire and was not in effect during 2011. In addition, the 2010 tax act reduced the employee's share of the Social Security payroll tax—from 6.2 percent to 4.2 percent—for one year; that provision was extended through 2012 by two subsequent laws, but it was not extended into 2013. The 2010 tax act also increased the exemption amounts for the alternative minimum tax (AMT) in both 2010 and 2011.[19]

The American Taxpayer Relief Act of 2012, which was enacted in January 2013, made permanent most of the major provisions of EGTRRA and JGTRRA—with significant exceptions for high-income taxpayers. Specifically, for taxpayers earning in excess of $400,000 (for individual filers) or $450,000 (for married people filing jointly), the lower tax rates originally enacted in 2001 expired as scheduled, and the top statutory tax rate of 39.6 percent was reinstated. Also, the tax rate for longterm capital gains and dividends was increased from 15 percent to 20 percent for those high-income taxpayers, and limitations on the use of personal exemptions and itemized deductions for taxpayers whose adjusted gross income was above $250,000 (for individual filers) or $300,000 (for joint filers) were reinstated. The act also permanently limited the reach of the alternative minimum tax and extended through 2017 the ARRA tax credits that were in effect in 2012. As noted above, the law did not extend the reduction in the payroll tax rate.

Also taking effect in 2013 were two new taxes on high-income taxpayers that were implemented under the Affordable Care Act. For taxpayers earning more than $200,000 (for individual filers) or $250,000 (for joint filers), the Medicare payroll tax rate was increased by 0.9 percentage points. In addition, a 3.8 percent surtax was imposed on the lesser of a taxpayer's investment income (from interest, dividends, capital gains realizations, and certain passive business activity) and total income over certain thresholds ($200,000 for individual filers and $250,000 for joint filers).

The Affordable Care Act also created tax subsidies (that took effect in 2014) for the purchase of health insurance through exchanges and an excise tax (that is scheduled to take effect in 2018) on certain health insurance plans with high premiums. CBO is still developing a methodology to incorporate the effects of those provisions of the Affordable Care Act in its distributional analyses.

Caveats About This Portion of the Analysis

Two important caveats apply to CBO's estimates of federal tax rates under 2013 tax rules. First, the analysis does not account for any shifts in the distribution of income between 2011 and 2013, which will not be known until detailed tax information becomes available. The further recovery of the economy might have resulted in uneven growth in incomes at different points in the income scale, which could affect tax rates for households in different income groups. Additionally, taxpayers probably changed their behavior in various ways in response to the changes in tax rules between 2011 and 2013. For example, higher-income taxpayers probably shifted some income from 2013 into 2012 in anticipation of the scheduled tax increases. Such shifts represent temporary changes in income, and holding incomes fixed, as this analysis does, may be a better way to measure the longterm effects of the tax changes. However, higher-income taxpayers probably also reduced their incomes in permanent ways because of the tax increases, and to the extent that is true, holding incomes fixed misstates the long-term effects of the tax changes.

Table 4. Average Federal Tax Rates, by before-Tax Income Group, 2011 and Projected under 2013 Law

Percent	2011	Projected Under 2013 Law	Change (Percentage points)
Lowest Quintile	1.9	2.9	1.0
Second Quintile	7.0	8.0	1.0
Middle Quintile	11.2	12.3	1.1
Fourth Quintile	15.2	16.4	1.2
Highest Quintile	23.4	25.5	2.1
All Households	17.6	19.3	1.7
81st to 90th Percentiles	18.6	19.8	1.2
91st to 95th Percentiles	21.1	22.3	1.2
96th to 99th Percentiles	24.3	25.4	1.1
Top 1 Percent	29.0	33.3	4.3

Source: Congressional Budget Office.

Notes: Average federal tax rates are calculated by dividing federal taxes by before-tax income.

Before-tax income is market income plus government transfers. Market income consists of labor income, business income, capital gains (profits realized from the sale of assets), capital income excluding capital gains, income received in retirement for past services, and other sources of income. Government transfers are cash payments and in-kind benefits from social insurance and other government assistance programs. Those transfers include payments and benefits from federal, state, and local governments.

Federal taxes include individual income taxes, payroll taxes, corporate income taxes, and excise taxes.

Federal tax rates for 2013 are calculated by applying individual income tax and payroll tax rules in place in 2013 to the income distribution observed in 2011.

Income groups are created by ranking households by before-tax income, adjusted for household size. Quintiles (fifths) contain equal numbers of people; percentiles (hundredths) contain equal numbers of people as well.

For more detailed definitions of income, see the appendix.

Second, CBO considered only the major changes to individual income and payroll taxes and did not incorporate minor changes to those taxes or any changes to corporate income taxes or excise taxes.[20] For example, under 2011 law, tax filers with qualifying investment properties could deduct 100 percent of their investment expenses. That full expensing provision (introduced in the Tax Relief, Unemployment Insurance Reauthorization, and Job Creation Act of 2010) expired at the end of 2012, and the depreciation schedule used for investments in 2013 was less generous than the full expensing in effect in

2011. Under the rules for 2013, depreciation deductions would have been smaller and taxable business income and taxes would therefore have been larger than the amounts reflected in CBO's analysis of 2011 data.

Federal Tax Rates under 2013 Tax Rules across the Income Scale

Holding the distribution of income constant and not incorporating any changes in taxpayers' behavior in response to the changes in tax rules, CBO estimates that the average federal tax rate for all households taken together would have been about 1.7 percentage points higher under 2013 tax rules than it was in 2011. The difference in federal tax rates would not have been uniform across the distribution of before-tax income, however: Average federal tax rates would have increased a little across much of the income distribution but sharply at the very top of the distribution (see Table 4).

CBO estimates that the average tax rate for all households except those in the top 1 percent of the distribution of before-tax income would have been approximately 1 percentage point higher under 2013 law than they were in 2011. The uniformity of that increase stems primarily from the rise in payroll tax rates after the temporary reduction in those rates expired at the end of 2012. Even with that increase, however, average federal tax rates for households outside of the top 1 percent would have been below the average rates for households in their income groups between 1979 and 2011.

In contrast, CBO estimates that households in the top percentile of the distribution of before-tax income would have faced an average tax rate that was 4.3 percentage points higher under 2013 tax law than it was in 2011 (33.3 percent versus 29.0 percent). That increase can be attributed to the higher tax rates for high-income households that resulted from the expiration of earlier tax reductions and from the additional taxes on high-income households enacted in the Affordable Care Act. The average rate for households in that income group in 2013 would have been close to the highest rate for that group between 1979 and 2011.

TRENDS IN HOUSEHOLD INCOME AND FEDERAL TAXES

The distributions of household income and federal taxes depend on economic conditions and tax laws—both of which have changed over time.

Changes in the distribution of after-tax income can be traced to changes in the distributions of market income, government transfers, and federal taxes.

Trends in Market Income

The growth in market income from 1979 to 2011 varied significantly across the income scale. Over the entire 33-year period, cumulative growth in inflation-adjusted market income was 16 percent for households in the bottom quintile, 16 percent for households in the next three quintiles taken together, and much greater for households in the top quintile, CBO estimates (see Figure 8). Specifically, cumulative growth in inflation-adjusted market income for households in the 81st through 99th percentiles was 56 percent over the period, and cumulative growth for households in the top 1 percent of the distribution was 174 percent over the period.

For households not in the top 1 percent of the income distribution, the composition of market income by source was relatively stable between 1979 and 2011. However, the composition of market income changed markedly over time for households in the top 1 percent (see Figure 9). Their labor income and business income grew especially rapidly—by more than 200 percent and 450 percent, respectively—while their capital income excluding capital gains grew by a comparatively modest 63 percent, CBO estimates. Realized capital gains for households in the top 1 percent of the income distribution increased by about 100 percent between 1979 and 2011. However, the year-to-year volatility of those gains means that cumulative growth differs dramatically depending on the precise period examined: Realized capital gains for this group increased by almost 500 percent between 1979 and 2007 and by 135 percent between 1979 and 2009.

Because of the volatile nature of capital gains realizations and their significance in the income of the highest-income households, shifts in the relative importance of other sources of income for that group can be seen more clearly by examining market income excluding capital gains. From 1979 through the early 2000s, the share of that income for the top 1 percent of households that came from capital income excluding capital gains fell by half—from about 40 percent to about 20 percent, CBO estimates (see Figure 10). The share of that income taking the form of capital income turned back up in the early 2000s and then dropped again in the late 2000s as capital income fell during the last recession. In contrast, the share of market income excluding capital gains for the top 1 percent of households that came from business income surged from 14 percent in 1979 to about 27 percent in 2011.

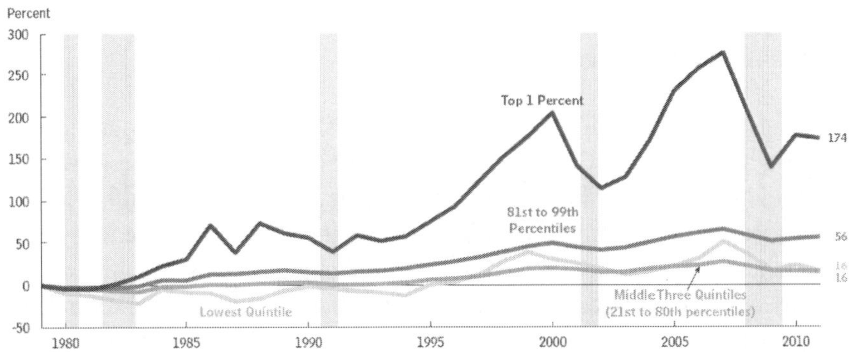

Source: Congressional Budget Office.

Notes: Market income consists of labor income, business income, capital gains (profits realized from the sale of assets), capital income excluding capital gains, income received in retirement for past services, and other sources of income. Government transfers are cash payments and in-kind benefits from social insurance and other government assistance programs. Those transfers include payments and benefits from federal, state, and local governments.

Income is converted to 2011 dollars using the personal consumption expenditures price index.

Income groups are created by ranking households by market income, adjusted for household size. Quintiles (fifths) contain equal numbers of people; percentiles (hundredths) contain equal numbers of people as well.

For more detailed definitions of income, see the appendix.

Figure 8. Cumulative Growth in Average Inflation-Adjusted Market Income, by Market Income Group, 1979 to 2011.

That shift in the composition of market income for households in the top 1 percent of the income distribution probably reflects, at least in part, significant changes in the organizational structure of businesses that have occurred over the past few decades. Following the Tax Reform Act of 1986, which lowered the top statutory tax rate on individual income below the top statutory tax rate on corporate income, many C corporations (which are taxed under the corporate income tax) were converted to S corporations (which pass corporate income through to their shareholders, where it is taxed under the individual income tax) or other types of entities not subject to the corporate income tax.[21] As a result, some income previously reported as capital gains and dividends (from C corporations) was instead reported as business income (from S corporations or other pass-through entities). That conversion also accelerated the realization of income, because profits of S corporations are required to be fully distributed to shareholders every year, whereas C corporations can retain their earnings. Business income jumped and capital income dropped over the 1986–1988 period as those conversions began, and the share of business income has continued to grow since then as more conversions occur and as new businesses are less likely to be set up as C corporations.

Trends in before-Tax Income

Together, market income and government transfers constitute before-tax income. Government transfers include cash transfers (such as Social Security benefits and unemployment insurance benefits) and in-kind benefits (such as Medicare and Medicaid benefits).[22] Those transfers have increased significantly during the past few decades and accrue disproportionately to low-income households, so the cumulative growth in before-tax income exceeds the cumulative growth in market income by the largest amount for income groups toward the bottom of the income distribution.

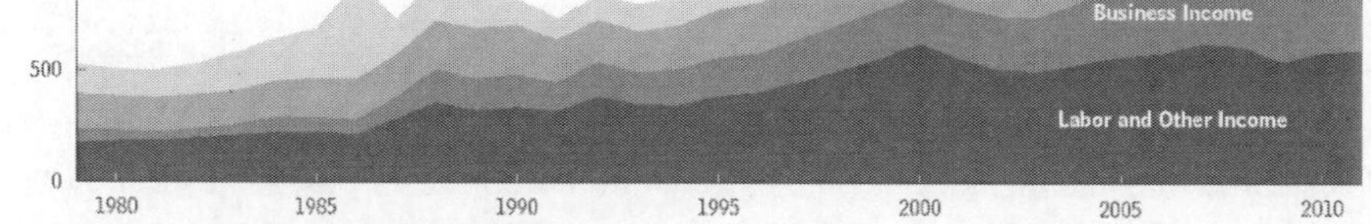

Source: Congressional Budget Office.

Notes: Other income includes income received in retirement for past services and other sources of income. Income is converted to 2011 dollars using the personal consumption expenditures price index. Income groups are created by ranking households by market income, adjusted for household size. For more detailed definitions of income, see the appendix.

Figure 9. Components of Inflation-Adjusted Market Income for the Top 1 Percent of Households, 1979 to 2011.

Between 1979 and 2011, the cumulative growth in inflation-adjusted before-tax income for households in the lowest quintile of before-tax income was 40 percent, CBO estimates (see Figure 11). For comparison, the cumulative growth in market income for households in the lowest quintile of market income was 16 percent over the same period.[23] For households in the middle three quintiles of before-tax income, the cumulative growth in inflation-adjusted before-tax income between 1979 and 2011 was 29 percent. That increase was greater than the cumulative growth in market income for households in the middle quintiles of market income but less than the cumulative growth in before-tax income for households in the lowest quintile of before-tax income.[24] For households in the 81st through 99th percentiles and in the top 1 percent, inflation-adjusted before-tax income increased by an estimated 59 percent and 175 percent, respectively, from 1979 to 2011. Those cumulative growth rates are only slightly larger than the ones observed for market income for households in the corresponding percentiles of the distribution of market income.

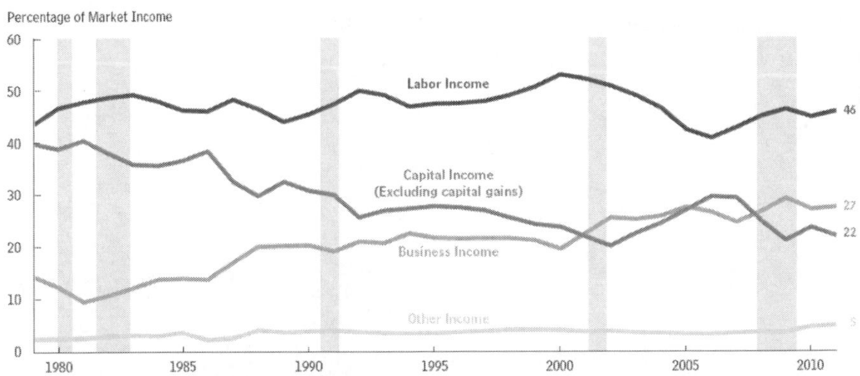

Source: Congressional Budget Office.

Notes: Other income includes income received in retirement for past services and other sources of income. Income groups are created by ranking households by market income, adjusted for household size. For more detailed definitions of income, see the appendix.

Figure 10. Shares of Market Income Excluding Capital Gains, by Source, for the Top 1 Percent of Households, 1979 to 2011.

Trends in Average Federal Tax Rates by Tax Source

In 2011, households paid, on average, 17.6 percent of their before-tax income in federal taxes, CBO estimates (see Figure 12). That overall average federal tax rate is the second lowest rate seen over the 1979–2011 period. After a drop of roughly 2 percentage points in the early 1980s, primarily because of the combined effects of tax law changes and two recessions, the overall average tax rate rose steadily from the mid-1980s through the 1990s, reaching a peak in 2000 of 22.7 percent. That rate fell again in the early 2000s, largely as a result of the tax legislation enacted in 2001 and 2003. The overall average tax rate climbed in the mid-2000s as economic conditions improved but then dropped between 2007 and 2008. The large decline between those years stemmed mostly from two factors: sharp decreases in capital gains and other capital income at the upper end of the income distribution during the financial crisis and start of the severe recession, and the Economic Stimulus Act of 2008, which provided a partially refundable payment of between $300 and $600 to people whose income was below certain thresholds. Additional changes in tax law and slow economic growth from 2009 through 2011 kept the overall average tax rate near its lowest level over the 33-year period examined here.

Individual Income Taxes

The average individual income tax rate (individual income taxes divided by before-tax income) in 2011 was an estimated 8.4 percent, which is below the average rate of 9.9 percent between 1979 and 2011. Over that period, the average individual income tax rate peaked at 11.9 percent in 1981, declined because of the reduction in tax rates enacted in 1981, and rose again after 1993 as a consequence of changes in tax law and rapidly rising incomes. After peaking at 11.7 percent in 2000, the rate fell to 8.3 percent in 2003 as a result of the 2001 and 2003 tax cuts and the 2001 recession and subsequent slow recovery. The rate dropped again in 2008 and 2009, to a low of 7.2 percent, because of declines in income and changes in tax law. At the end of 2010, the Making Work Pay tax credit, a refundable credit of up to $400 for a single tax filer or $800 for a married couple, expired. Primarily as a result of that expiration, the average individual income tax rate increased between 2010 and 2011.

Payroll Taxes

Between 1979 and 1991, the average payroll tax rate rose steadily from 6.8 percent to a high of 8.5 percent, mostly because of legislated increases in the Social Security payroll tax rate and increases in the maximum earnings subject to that tax.[25]

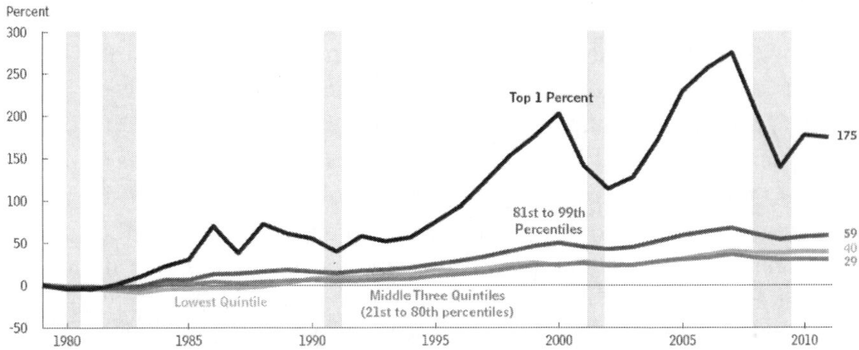

Source: Congressional Budget Office.

Notes: Before-tax income is market income plus government transfers. Market income consists of labor income, business income, capital gains (profits realized from the sale of assets), capital income excluding capital gains, income received in retirement for past services, and other sources of income. Government transfers are cash payments and in-kind benefits from social insurance and other government assistance programs. Those transfers include payments and benefits from federal, state, and local governments.

Income is converted to 2011 dollars using the personal consumption expenditures price index.

Income groups are created by ranking households by before-tax income, adjusted for household size. Quintiles (fifths) contain equal numbers of people; percentiles (hundredths) contain equal numbers of people as well.

For more detailed definitions of income, see the appendix.

Figure 11. Cumulative Growth in Average Inflation-Adjusted Before-Tax Income, by Before-Tax Income Group, 1979 to 2011.

The payroll tax rate declined slightly in the late 1990s as labor income grew more slowly than other income sources and as earnings above the maximum subject to Social Security taxes grew more rapidly than earnings below that amount. The 2001 recession and slow recovery reversed those trends, leading the tax rate to rise a bit in the early 2000s. The rate resumed its decline in the mid-2000s when economic growth picked up, before climbing in 2008 and 2009 as the recession caused nonlabor income to fall more sharply than labor income and caused earnings above the maximum subject to Social Security taxes to fall more than earnings below that amount. The Tax Relief, Unemployment Insurance Reauthorization, and Job Creation Act of 2010 reduced the employee's share of Social Security payroll taxes by 2 percentage points (from 6.2 percent to 4.2 percent), which decreased the average payroll tax rate to 6.7 percent in 2011. That rate was the lowest observed over the 1979–2011 period.

Corporate Taxes

The average corporate income tax rate declined significantly in the early 1980s and was then fairly steady over the next two decades, with some slight shifts that generally corresponded to economic expansions and contractions. After the 2001 recession, strong growth in corporate profits pushed the corporate income tax rate up through the mid-2000s. The rate then fell by more than half between 2006 and 2009 because of the sharp drop in corporate profits during the most recent recession. In 2011, the average corporate income tax rate was 1.9 percent, CBO estimates, close to the values seen in each year since 2007.

Excise Taxes

Unlike tax rates for the other revenue sources, the average excise tax rate was fairly stable over the entire 1979–2011 period. In 2011, the average excise tax rate was an estimated 0.7 percent.

Trends in Average Federal Tax Rates by before-Tax Income Group

For all of the income groups considered in this report, average federal tax rates in 2011 were below their averages over the preceding three decades (see Figure 2). For households in the bottom quintile of before-tax income, the average federal tax rate in 2011 was 4.6 percentage points lower than the average rate for that quintile over the 1979–2011 period, CBO estimates. For households in the middle three quintiles of before-tax income taken together, the average tax rate in 2011 was also 4.6 percentage points below the average for those 33 years. For households in the 81st through 99th percentiles and households in the top 1 percent of the income distribution, average tax rates in 2011 were lower than the average rates for those groups over the 1979– 2011 period but not by as much—by 2.6 percentage points and 1.4 percentage points, respectively.

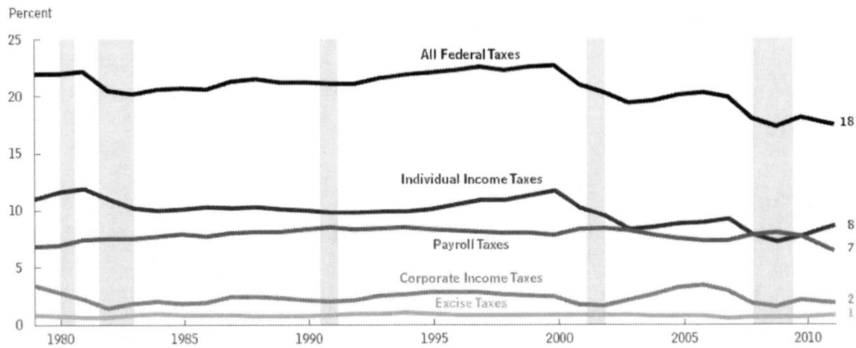

Source: Congressional Budget Office.

Notes: Average federal tax rates are calculated by dividing federal taxes by before-tax income.

Before-tax income is market income plus government transfers. Market income consists of labor income, business income, capital gains (profits realized from the sale of assets), capital income excluding capital gains, income received in retirement for past services, and other sources of income. Government transfers are cash payments and in-kind benefits from social insurance and other government assistance programs. Those transfers include payments and benefits from federal, state, and local governments.

For more detailed definitions of income, see the appendix.

Figure 12. Average Federal Tax Rates, by Tax Source, 1979 to 2011.

Changes to federal tax rules between 2011 and 2013 pushed average federal tax rates higher, especially among the highest-income households. The top statutory income tax rate increased in 2013 from 35 percent to 39.6 percent. In addition, the Social Security payroll tax rate reverted to its previous, higher level in 2013 after a temporary reduction in 2011 and 2012. Moreover, two new taxes on high-income taxpayers took effect in 2013. Yet, even with the increases in average tax rates in 2013, CBO estimates that those rates would have been lower for most income groups than they were in 2007, the year before the most recent recession began. The exception to that pattern is in the top income percentile, which would have had an average federal tax rate in 2013 that was much higher than it was in the years immediately before the recession.

Lowest Quintile

Between 1984 and 2007, the average federal tax rate for households in the lowest quintile of the distribution of before-tax income declined fairly steadily. Expansions of the earned income tax credit pushed down the average income tax rate for this group, especially in the 1990s, while increases in the average payroll tax rate were a partially offsetting factor. Between 2007 and 2008, the average tax rate for this group dropped markedly, largely as a result of the creation of the Making Work Pay tax credit and an expansion of the earned income and child tax credits. The average tax rate for this group increased from 2009 to 2011, mainly because of the expiration of the Making Work Pay tax credit; the temporary reduction in the employee's share of the Social Security payroll tax provided a partial offset. The average tax rate for this group was 1.9 percent in 2011, CBO estimates, compared with an average of 6.5 percent during the entire 1979–2011 period.

The significant changes in individual income taxes and payroll taxes between 2011 and 2013 would have generated an increase in the average federal tax rate for this group (holding the distribution of income constant) of approximately 1 percentage point, CBO estimates. The resulting average tax rate of 2.9 percent in 2013 would still have been well below the average for the preceding decades.

Middle Quintiles

Households in the middle three quintiles of before-tax income, taken as a group, experienced a decline in their average tax rate of almost 7 percentage points over the 1979–2011 period, from 19.1 percent in 1979 to 12.2 percent in 2011, CBO estimates. That decline was caused primarily by a drop in individual income taxes.

Specifically, the average tax rate for the middle three income quintiles fell somewhat in the early 1980s and then fluctuated within a fairly narrow range during the rest of the 1980s and the 1990s. Between 2000 and 2003, the rate declined by 3 percentage points, reflecting numerous changes in law—particularly the expansion of the child tax credit, reductions in tax rates, and increases in the standard deduction for married couples. The average tax rate for this group then edged up between 2003 and 2007 before falling by nearly 3 percentage points from 2007 to 2009. The estimated rate of 12.0 percent in 2009 was the lowest since at least 1979. Between 2009 and 2011, the average tax rate for the middle three income quintiles stayed near that low point.

Because of changes in tax provisions between 2011 and 2013, CBO estimates that the average federal tax rate for this group would have been 13.3 percent in 2013 (based on the distribution of income in 2011). That rate would still have been well below the average of 16.7 percent from 1979 through 2011.

81st Through 99th Percentiles

The average federal tax rate for households in the 81st through 99th percentiles of the distribution of before-tax income decreased in the early 1980s and then increased a little, on balance, during the rest of that decade and the 1990s. The rate then dropped nearly 3 percentage points between 2000 and 2003, rose modestly from 2003 to 2007, and fell again from 2007 to 2009. Its 2009 value of 21.1 percent was the lowest since at least 1979. Between 2009 and 2011, the rate changed only slightly.

Given the changes in tax provisions between 2011 and 2013, the average federal tax rate for this group in 2013 (based on the 2011 distribution of income) would have been 22.4 percent, CBO estimates—below its 1979–2011 average of 23.8 percent.

Top 1 Percent

The average federal tax rate for households in the top 1 percent of the distribution of before-tax income has followed a very different pattern than the average tax rates for other income groups. The average tax rate for this group fell sharply between 1979 and 1986, primarily because of changes in tax law, and reversed that decline between 1986 and 1995, when it peaked at 35.3 percent. The rate fell again between 1995 and 2008 and edged up, on balance, between 2008 and 2011. In 2011, the average tax rate for households in the top 1 percent of the income distribution was 29.0 percent, CBO estimates—near the average for the full 1979–2011 period of 30.4 percent, higher than the 28.2 percent average for the 1980s, and lower than the 32.6 percent average for the 1990s.

CBO estimates that the average federal tax rate for households in this income group would have increased to 33.3 percent in 2013 because of changes in tax provisions (and holding the distribution of income constant between 2011 and 2013, as discussed above). That rate would have been nearly 3 percentage points above the 1979–2011 average for this group.

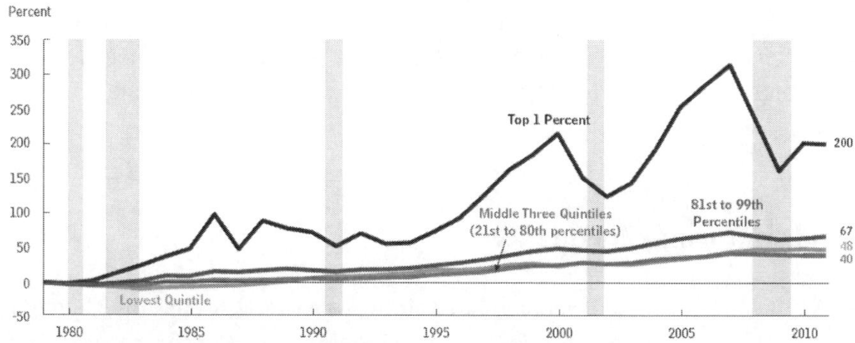

Source: Congressional Budget Office.

Notes: After-tax income is before-tax income minus federal taxes.

Before-tax income is market income plus government transfers. Market income consists of labor income, business income, capital gains (profits realized from the sale of assets), capital income excluding capital gains, income received in retirement for past services, and other sources of income. Government transfers are cash payments and in-kind benefits from social insurance and other government assistance programs. Those transfers include payments and benefits from federal, state, and local governments. Federal taxes include individual income taxes, payroll taxes, corporate income taxes, and excise taxes.

Income is converted to 2011 dollars using the personal consumption expenditures price index.

Income groups are created by ranking households by before-tax income, adjusted for household size. Quintiles (fifths) contain equal numbers of people; percentiles (hundredths) contain equal numbers of people as well.

For more detailed definitions of income, see the appendix.

Figure 13. Cumulative Growth in Average Inflation-Adjusted After-Tax Income, by Before-Tax Income Group, 1979 to 2011.

Trends in after-Tax Income

Changes in economic conditions, government transfer programs, and federal tax laws have resulted in after-tax income growing at different rates across the income spectrum over time. For households in the lowest quintile of before-tax income, inflation-adjusted after-tax income was 48 percent higher in 2011 than it was in 1979, CBO estimates. Cumulative growth in the inflation-adjusted after-tax income of households in the 21st to 80th percentiles, the 81st to 99th percentiles, and the top 1 percent of the before-tax income distribution was an estimated 40 percent, 67 percent, and 200 percent, respectively (see Figure 13).[26] Each of those percentage increases in after-tax income exceeds the percentage increases in before-tax income for the corresponding income groups because the average federal tax rate for each income group was lower in 2011 than in 1979.

Trends in Income Inequality

As the distributions of income have shifted over time, so has the degree of inequality in market income, before-tax income, and after-tax income.[27] A standard measure of income inequality is the Gini index, which summarizes an entire distribution in a single number that ranges from zero to one. A value of zero means that income is distributed equally among all income groups, while a value of one indicates that all of the income is received by the highest-income group and none is received by any of the lower-income groups. Inequality of all three measures of income increased between 1979 and 2011, according to CBO's estimates (see Figure 15).[28]

Inequality as measured by the Gini index is consistently lower for after-tax income than for before-tax income and consistently lower for before-tax income than for market income.[29] Government transfers reduce income inequality because the transfers received by lower-income households are larger relative to their market income than are the transfers received by higher-income households. Federal taxes also reduce income inequality, because the taxes paid by higher-income households are larger relative to their before-tax income than are the taxes paid by lower-income households. The equalizing effects of government transfers were significantly larger than the equalizing effects of federal taxes from 1979 to 2011.

The effect of government transfers on income inequality varies across economic expansions and contractions because such transfers tend to decline when the economy is strong and to increase when the economy is weak—because of both automatic changes in benefits from some programs (such as unemployment insurance) and legislated changes in response to fluctuating economic conditions. During the most recent recession, the percentage decline in the Gini index attributable to government transfers increased from 15 percent in 2007 to 20 percent in 2009, CBO estimates (see Figure 15).[30] That additional reduction in inequality is attributable primarily to an automatic increase in unemployment insurance benefits and significant legislated expansions of those benefits and benefits from the Supplemental Nutrition Assistance Program (see Box 2).[31]

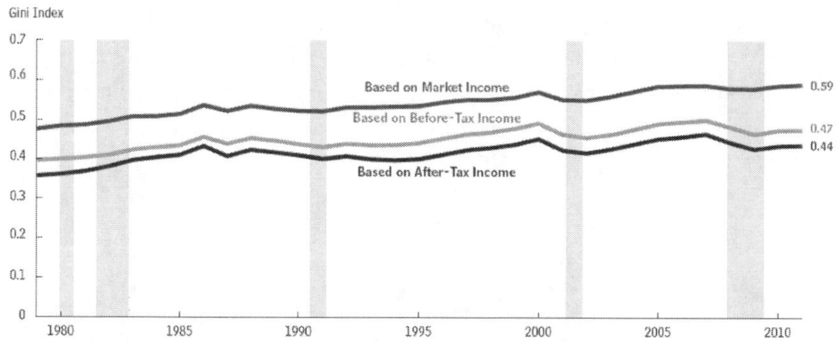

Source: Congressional Budget Office.

Notes: The Gini index is a measure of income inequality that ranges from zero (the most equal distribution) to one (the least equal distribution). Gini indexes are calculated using income measures adjusted for household size.

Market income consists of labor income, business income, capital gains (profits realized from the sale of assets), capital income excluding capital gains, income received in retirement for past services, and other sources of income.

Before-tax income is market income plus government transfers. Government transfers are cash payments and in-kind benefits from social insurance and other government assistance programs. Those transfers include payments and benefits from federal, state, and local governments.

After-tax income is before-tax income minus federal taxes. Federal taxes include individual income taxes, payroll taxes, corporate income taxes, and excise taxes.

For more detailed definitions of income, see the appendix.

Figure 14. Gini Indexes Based on Market, Before-Tax, and After-Tax Income, 1979 to 2011.

The effect of federal taxes on income inequality was quite stable between the mid-1990s and 2011 because of two trends that were roughly offsetting.[32] First, the share of federal taxes paid by higher-income households increased more than the share of income earned by that group. For example, the share of before-tax income received by households in the top quintile increased by 2.5 percentage points between 1995 and 2011, whereas the share of federal taxes paid by those households increased by 7.5 percentage points over that period, CBO estimates. Second, average federal tax rates across the income spectrum decreased. With federal taxes becoming both more progressive and smaller relative to before-tax income between the mid-1990s and 2011, those taxes had roughly the same effect in reducing income inequality throughout that period.

The changes in tax provisions that took effect between 2011 and 2013 would have made federal taxes more progressive. Holding all else equal, those changes would have increased the effect of federal taxes in reducing income inequality.

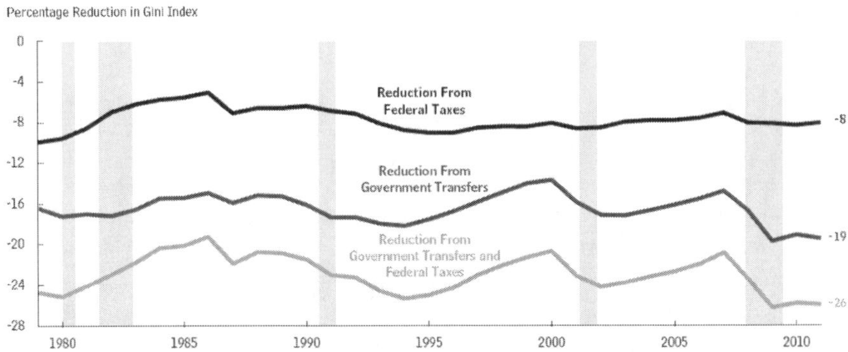

Source: Congressional Budget Office.

Notes: The Gini index is a measure of income inequality that ranges from zero (the most equal distribution) to one (the least equal distribution). Gini indexes are calculated using income measures adjusted for household size.

Government transfers are cash payments and in-kind benefits from social insurance and other government assistance programs.

Those transfers include payments and benefits from federal, state, and local governments.

Federal taxes include individual income taxes, payroll taxes, corporate income taxes, and excise taxes.

Figure 15. Reduction in Income Inequality From Government Transfers and Federal Taxes, 1979 to 2011.

Box 2. Government Transfers and Federal Taxes Over Time

This Congressional Budget Office (CBO) report examines three measures of income: market income, before-tax income, and after-tax income. Market income consists mainly of labor income, business income, capital income (including realized capital gains), and retirement income. Before-tax income is market income plus government transfers, which are made up of cash payments and in-kind benefits from federal, state, and local governments.

The average tax rate equals tax obligations divided by before-tax income, which is a proxy for the income available to pay those obligations. After-tax income is before-tax income minus federal (but not state and local) taxes.

Government transfers and federal taxes both compress the distribution of income. In general, transfers increase income more toward the bottom of the distribution, and federal taxes reduce income more toward the top of the distribution.

Households in the highest quintile (or fifth) of the income distribution ranked by market income receive little transfer income and pay a significant share of their market income in federal taxes (see the figure).[1] In 2011, CBO estimates, households in that group had average market income of $240,800 and average after-tax income of $188,300. In contrast, households in the lowest quintile ranked by market income pay little in taxes but receive a significant amount in transfers. In 2011, CBO estimates, households in that group had average market income of $7,900 and average after-tax income of $31,600. Roughly two-thirds of the transfer income for those households came from Social Security and Medicare. For households in the middle quintile, taxes and transfers (predominantly from Social Security and Medicare) nearly offset each other.

Market income and after-tax income evolved in markedly different ways during the recent recession and slow recovery. Between 2007 and 2011, after-tax income fell by less than market income across the income spectrum, with especially large differences in the bottom half of the distribution by market income. In those four years, inflation-adjusted market income for households in the lowest quintile of market income fell by 23 percent, but after-tax income for that group rose by 5 percent. Households in the middle quintile saw their market income fall by 11 percent but their after-tax income decrease by only 3 percent. The drop in market income and rise in transfers for this group caused their after-tax income to exceed their market income since 2008. That reverses the previous pattern: Between 1979 and 2007, federal taxes paid by this group were a little larger than the transfers they received, so their after-tax income was less than their market income, on average. For households in the highest quintile of market income, the difference between their change in market income and their change in after-tax income between 2007 and 2011 was much smaller: Market income declined by 14 percent, and after-tax income fell by 12 percent.

Over the 1979–2011 period, the cumulative growth in after-tax income was larger than the cumulative growth in market income for all income groups. For the lowest quintile and middle quintiles of market income, government transfers rose more rapidly than market income and average federal tax rates declined, pushing up after-tax income relative to market income. Specifically, average market income among households in the lowest income quintile increased by an estimated 16 percent between 1979 and 2011, whereas average after-tax income for those households increased by 72 percent; the corresponding increases for households in the middle income quintile were 9 percent and 33 percent. For the highest quintile of market income, government transfers are not a significant factor, but average federal tax rates declined for this group as well. Therefore, among households in the highest income quintile, market income rose by 77 percent and after-tax income rose by 87 percent over that period.

1. In this section of CBO's analysis, income groups for both market income and after-tax income are based on households ranked by market income.

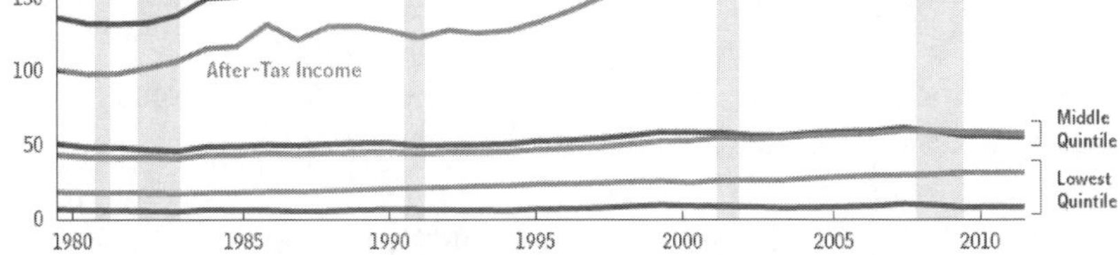

Source: Congressional Budget Office.

Notes: Market income consists of labor income, business income, capital gains (profits realized from the sale of assets), capital income excluding capital gains, income received in retirement for past services, and other sources of income.

After-tax income is market income plus government transfers minus federal taxes.

Government transfers are cash payments and in-kind benefits from social insurance and other government assistance programs. Those transfers include payments and benefits from federal, state, and local governments.

Federal taxes include individual income taxes, payroll taxes, corporate income taxes, and excise taxes. Income is adjusted for inflation using the personal consumption expenditure price index.

Income groups are created by ranking households by market income, adjusted for household size. Quintiles (fifths) contain equal numbers of people.

For more detailed definitions of income, see the appendix.

Average Market and After-Tax Income for Households in Selected Market Income Groups, 1979 to 2011.

APPENDIX: DATA AND METHODS

In this report, the Congressional Budget Office (CBO) examines the distribution of household income and federal tax rates, focusing on data from calendar year 2011. The current analysis builds on earlier CBO analyses, the most recent of which covered the period from 1979 through 2010.[1]

Data Sources on Household Income

Information on household income for this analysis came from two primary sources: the Internal Revenue Service's Statistics of Income (SOI) and the Census Bureau's Current Population Survey (CPS). The core data came from the SOI, a nationally representative sample of individual income tax returns. The number of returns sampled grew over the time period studied, ranging from roughly 90,000 in some of the early years to more than 300,000 in the later years. CBO used the full Individual Income Tax file, which is more detailed than the public-use version of the file. The agency supplemented those data with data from the CPS's Annual Social and Economic Supplement; those data identify demographic characteristics and income for a large sample of households.

Both the SOI and the CPS lack important information needed for estimating and comparing after-tax household income over time. The SOI does not include information about people who do not file federal tax returns, and it does not report all income from government cash transfer programs. It also offers no information on the receipt of in-kind transfers and benefits, and it is organized by tax filing units rather than by households. The CPS lacks detailed information on high-income households, it does not report capital gains, it underreports other income from capital, and it lacks information on the deductions and adjustments necessary to compute taxes.

Together, however, the two sources can form a more complete picture. To overcome limitations in each source of data, CBO statistically matched SOI records to corresponding CPS records on the basis of demographic characteristics and income. Each pairing resulted in a new record that took on the demographic characteristics of the CPS record and the income reported in the SOI. (Some types of income—certain transfers and in-kind benefits, for example—appear only in the CPS; their values were drawn directly from that survey.) Because some households are not required to file tax returns, the SOI does not have data on every household in the nation. To create a sample that was representative of the entire population, once all SOI records were matched to CPS records, the remaining CPS records were recorded as nonfiling households and their income values were taken directly from the CPS.

Allocation of Taxes to Households

CBO allocated individual income taxes and the employee's share of payroll taxes to the households paying those taxes directly.[2] The agency also allocated the employer's share of payroll taxes to employees because employers appear to pass on their share of payroll taxes to employees by paying lower wages than they would otherwise pay.[3] Therefore, CBO also added the employer's share of payroll taxes to households' earnings in calculating before-tax income.

CBO allocated excise taxes to households according to their consumption of taxed goods and services (such as gasoline, tobacco, and alcohol). Excise taxes on intermediate goods, which are paid by businesses, were attributed to households in proportion to their overall consumption. CBO assumed that each household's spending on taxed goods and services was the same as that reported in the Bureau of Labor Statistics' Consumer Expenditure Survey for a household with comparable income and other characteristics.

Far less consensus exists about how to allocate corporate income taxes (and taxes on capital income generally). In this analysis, CBO allocated 75 percent of corporate income taxes to owners of capital in proportion to their income from interest, dividends, rents, and adjusted capital gains; the adjustment smoothes out large year-to-year variations in actual realized gains by scaling them to an estimate of their long-term historical level given the size of the economy and the tax rate that applies to them.[4] CBO allocated the remaining 25 percent of corporate income taxes to workers in proportion to their labor income.

Measures of Income

This analysis uses three measures of household income: market income; market income plus government transfers (before-tax income); and market income plus government transfers minus federal taxes (after-tax income).

Market income consists of the following components:

- *Labor Income.* Cash wages and salaries, including amounts allocated by employees to 401(k) plans; employer-paid health insurance premiums; the employer's share of Social Security, Medicare, and federal unemployment insurance payroll taxes; and the share of corporate income taxes borne by workers.
- *Business Income.* Net income from businesses and farms operated solely by their owners, partnership income, and income from S corporations.
- *Capital Gains.* Profits realized from the sale of assets, excluding increases in the value of assets that have not been realized through sales.[5]
- *Capital Income Excluding Capital Gains.* Taxable and tax-exempt interest, dividends paid by corporations (but not dividends paid by S corporations, which are considered part of business income), positive rental income, and the share of corporate income taxes borne by owners of capital.
- *Other Income.* Income received in retirement for past services or from other sources.[6]

Government transfers consist of the cost of two types of benefits:

- *Cash.* Payments from Social Security, unemployment insurance, Supplemental Security Income, Temporary Assistance for Needy Families (and its predecessor, Aid to Families With Dependent Children), veterans' programs, workers' compensation, and state and local government assistance programs.
- *In-Kind Benefits.* The cost of Supplemental Nutrition Assistance Program vouchers (popularly known as food stamps); school lunches

and breakfasts; housing assistance; energy assistance; and benefits provided by Medicare, Medicaid, and the Children's Health Insurance Program.[7]

This report focuses on annual income. It does not assess trends in the distribution of other measures of economic well-being, such as household income measured over longer periods, household consumption, or household wealth.[8] Because household income varies over time, a household in a given segment of the income distribution in one year could be in a different segment in another year.

Adjusting Income for Differences among Households

CBO used the household as the unit of analysis for this report. A household consists of the people who share a housing unit, regardless of their relationship. Analyzing income and taxes on a household basis is most useful if households make joint economic decisions, which is probably true in most cases but not all (such as group houses). A household can consist of more than one taxpaying unit, such as a married couple living with an adult child.

Households with identical income can differ in ways that affect their economic status. A larger household generally needs more income to support a given standard of living than a smaller one does. However, economies of scale in some types of consumption—housing, in particular—can mean that two people generally do not need twice the income to live as well as one person who lives alone.

Therefore, to rank households by their standard of living, it is probably appropriate to divide household income by an adjustment factor that is between 1 (which would result only in household income and would not capture the greater needs of larger households) and the number of people in the household (which would produce household income per person and would not capture the benefits of shared consumption). CBO chose to adjust for household size by dividing household income by the square root of the number of people in the household, counting adults and children equally.[9] Households were then ranked by adjusted income and grouped into quintiles (or fifths) of equal numbers of people. Because household sizes vary, different quintiles generally have slightly different numbers of households.

Adjusting income for other differences in circumstances that affect a household's standard of living also could be desirable. For example, the prices of goods and services vary geographically, and households can incur different costs associated with working—for commuting and child care expenses, for example—depending on how many members are employed. CBO did not adjust for any such additional differences.

Types of Households

Changes in the composition of household types—and household sizes—can affect the distribution of income over time. Supplemental tables, available online, show household income and average federal tax rates for three types of households: those with members under age 18 (households with children), those headed by a person age 65 or older and with no members under age 18 (elderly childless households), and all others (nonelderly childless households). The tables group households into quintiles by their position in the income distribution across the full population, not by their position in the income distribution for each type of household.

End Notes

[1] In this analysis, federal taxes are the amount a household owes on the basis of income received in that year, regardless of when the taxes are paid. The term "paid" is used throughout the report for simplicity.

[2] As used in this report, the Affordable Care Act comprises the Patient Protection and Affordable Care Act (Public Law 111-148), the health care provisions of the Health Care and Education Reconciliation Act of 2010 (P.L. 111-152), and the effects of subsequent judicial decisions, statutory changes, and administrative actions.

[3] Although tax law changed significantly again in 2014, owing largely to other provisions of the Affordable Care Act, CBO is still developing a methodology to incorporate the effects of those changes in its distributional analyses.

[4] CBO chose 1979 as a starting point for the analysis because it is the earliest year for which the Census Bureau provides consistent estimates of some measures of income. The beginning and end points of the analysis—1979 and 2011—were quite different in terms of economic activity; 1979 was a peak year for the economy right before a recession, whereas 2011 was a year in which the economy was still slowly recovering from the deep recession that began in 2007.

[5] Taxes and transfers can affect households' market income by creating incentives for people to change their behavior. If an additional dollar earned or saved leads to reductions in transfers or increases in taxes, then the after-tax return from working and saving is reduced, which may cause people to work or save less. However, those changes in transfers and taxes also reduce after-tax income, which may cause people to work or save more. In this analysis,

CBO did not attempt to adjust market income to account for those behavioral effects of transfers and taxes.

[6] See the appendix for more details on the other sources of income included in market income.

[7] Transfers as measured in this report do not equal total government spending on the transfer programs included in the analysis. The values of most transfers are based on amounts reported in the Census Bureau's Current Population Survey. The values of transfers from Medicare, Medicaid, and the Children's Health Insurance Program are based on the Census Bureau's estimate of the government's average cost of providing those benefits. In addition, because some transfers go to recipients outside the scope of the survey data collected by the Census Bureau and because some recipients misreport the amount of transfer payments they receive, the total amount of government transfers observed in the data used here is lower than the total amount the government spends through those transfer programs. See the appendix for more details.

[8] For this analysis, federal taxes include individual income taxes, payroll taxes, corporate income taxes, and excise taxes, which together accounted for approximately 92 percent of all federal revenues in fiscal year 2011. Revenues from states' deposits for unemployment insurance, estate and gift taxes, miscellaneous fees and fines, and net income earned by the Federal Reserve, which make up the remaining 8 percent, are not allocated to households in this analysis, mainly because it is uncertain to which households those revenue sources should be attributed.

[9] Dollar amounts presented in this report are generally rounded to the nearest hundred.

[10] Differences between the values presented in this section and those presented in Table 1 stem from differences in the income measure by which households are ranked. In Table 1, households are ranked by before-tax income, which includes income from government transfer programs, including Social Security and Medicare; in this section, households are ranked by market income, which excludes income from transfer programs. The different ranking means that the households in the lowest quintile of before-tax income are not the same as those in the lowest quintile of market income.

[11] CBO recently undertook a more comprehensive analysis of the distribution of federal spending in 2006. Although that study used a similar methodology to the one used in this report, it differed in some important respects, most notably by adjusting the amount of transfer income reported in survey data to match the budgetary totals reported in the Treasury Department's *Monthly Treasury Statements*. The data used in this report are not aligned to budgetary totals and, because of underreporting of transfer income in surveys, do not capture the full effects of government transfers on household income. For more details, see Congressional Budget Office, *The Distribution of Federal Spending and Taxes in 2006* (November 2013), www.cbo.gov/publication/44698.

[12] Transfers increase income most significantly for households at the bottom of the income distribution. Therefore, when households are ranked by before-tax income, which includes government transfers, households that are in the lowest market income quintile may be moved into higher before-tax income quintiles. Conversely, households in higher market income quintiles that receive less in transfers may move into lower before-tax income quintiles. Because of that reranking, income groups based on before-tax income are not directly comparable with income groups based on market income.

[13] Because of the complexity of estimating state and local taxes for individual households, this report considers federal taxes only. Researchers differ about whether state and local taxes are, on net, regressive, proportional, or slightly progressive, but most agree that state and local taxes are less progressive than federal taxes. For estimates of the distribution of state

and local taxes, see Gerald Prante and Scott A. Hodge, *The Distribution of Tax and Spending Policies in the United States,* Special Report No. 211 (Tax Foundation, November 2013), http://taxfoundation.org/ article/distribution-tax-and-spending-policies-united-states; and Carl Davis and others, *Who Pays? A Distributional Analysis of the Tax Systems in All 50 States*, 3rd ed. (Institute on Taxation and Economic Policy, November 2009), http://tinyurl.com/ke3abe2.

[14] In the federal budget, the refundable portion of individual income tax credits is treated as an outlay. In this analysis, CBO considers the refundable portion of certain individual income tax credits— the earned income tax credit and the child tax credit—to be a negative tax liability rather than a federal outlay.

[15] In addition to varying *across* income groups, average tax rates can vary significantly *within* each income group. The variation within income groups is attributable to several factors, including differences in the composition of income, family structure, and use of tax preferences, as well as the progressive rate structure. For more discussion of the variation in average tax rates within income groups, see Congressional Budget Office, *The Distribution of Household Income and Federal Taxes, 2010* (December 2013), www.cbo.gov/publication /44604.

[16] CBO allocates 75 percent of the corporate income tax to households in proportion to their share of capital income and 25 percent to households in proportion to their share of labor income. For more discussion of the incidence of the corporate income tax, see Congressional Budget Office, *The Distribution of Household Income and Federal Taxes, 2008 and 2009* (July 2012), www.cbo.gov/publication/43373. For more discussion of the adjustments made to realized capital gains when allocating the corporate tax to households, see the appendix.

[17] Differences in the distributions of after-tax income shown in Figure 6 and Figure 7 are attributable to differences in the income measure used to rank households in the two figures. Households are ranked by before-tax income adjusted for household size in Figure 6 and market income adjusted for household size in Figure 7.

[18] Specifically, CBO deflated the dollar amounts specified in the 2013 tax rules by the nominal growth in per capita income between 2011 and 2013 (approximately 4.5 percent) and then applied those adjusted tax parameters to 2011 incomes. The resulting estimated changes in average tax rates thus reflect both the effects of changes in tax law and a small amount of "bracket creep" to the extent that incomes grew faster than the inflation-indexed tax parameters. Those adjustments were applied only to the individual income tax and the payroll tax; the corporate income tax rates and excise tax rates in effect in 2011 were assumed to be unchanged in 2013.

[19] The AMT is a parallel income tax system with fewer exemptions, deductions, credits, and rates than the regular income tax. Households must calculate the amount they owe under both the AMT and the regular income tax and pay the larger of the two amounts.

[20] The American Taxpayer Relief Act of 2012 significantly modified estate and gift tax rules for 2013 relative to the rules specified for that year under prior law, increasing the exemption amount from $1 million to $5.25 million and reducing the top tax rate from 55 percent to 40 percent. Estate and gift taxes are not included in this analysis, either for 2013 or for earlier years. However, those taxes were included in a previous CBO report; see *The Distribution of Federal Spending and Taxes in 2006* (November 2013), www.cbo.gov/publication /44698.

[21] For more details on that shift, see *Taxing Businesses Through the Individual Income Tax* (December 2012), www.cbo.gov/ publication/43750.

[22] The government transfers included in before-tax income are mostly federal transfers, but they also include transfers from state and local governments—the largest of which is states' share of the cost of Medicaid benefits.

[23] Because households receive different amounts of government transfers, the ranking of households based on market income differs from the ranking of households based on before-tax income. As a result, income groups that are based on ranking households by before-tax income include different households than the corresponding groups that are based on ranking households by market income.

[24] CBO recently examined trends in federal spending for means-tested transfer programs. See *Growth in Means-Tested Programs and Tax Credits for Low-Income Households* (February 2013), www.cbo.gov/publication/43934.

[25] The payroll tax rate is calculated as payroll taxes divided by total before-tax income. Therefore, when the amount of before-tax income subject to the tax rises, the average payroll tax rate increases as well.

[26] Those cumulative growth figures are equivalent to average annual growth rates over the 33-year period of 1.2 percent, 1.1 percent, 1.6 percent, and 3.5 percent, respectively.

[27] A significant body of research has examined changes in U.S. income inequality over time, using various data sources and measures of income. For example, Thomas Piketty and Emmanuel Saez rely on income tax data from the Internal Revenue Service's Statistics of Income; see Piketty and Saez, "Income Inequality in the United States, 1913–1998," *Quarterly Journal of Economics*, vol. 118, no. 1 (February 2003), pp. 1–39, http://eml.berkeley.edu/~saez/pikettyqje.pdf. Timothy M. Smeeding and Jeffrey P. Thompson rely on the Federal Reserve's Survey of Consumer Finances; see Smeeding and Thompson, "Recent Trends in Income Inequality," in Herwig Immervoll, Andreas Peichl, and Konstantinos Tatsiramos, eds.,*Who Loses in the Downturn? Economic Crisis, Employment, and Income Distribution,* vol. 32 (Research in Labor Economics), pp.1–50, http://tinyurl.com/qdk92x4. Philip Armour, Richard V. Burkhauser, and Jeff Larrimore rely on the Census Bureau's Current Population Survey; see Armour, Burkhauser, and Larrimore, *Levels and Trends in United States Income and Its Distribution: A Crosswalk From Market Income Towards a Comprehensive Haig-Simons Income Approach*, Working Paper 19110 (National Bureau of Economic Research, June 2013), www.nber.org/papers/w19110.

[28] Gini indexes in this report are calculated on the basis of incomes adjusted for household size. For a more detailed discussion of CBO's approach to calculating Gini indexes, see *Trends in the Distribution of Household Income Between 1979 and 2007* (October 2011), www.cbo.gov/publication/42729.

[29] Gini indexes for market, before-tax, and after-tax income reflect rankings of households based on those income measures. Therefore, some of the differences between the Gini indexes are attributable to the reranking of households across the indexes.

[30] Transfers as measured in this report do not equal total government spending on the transfers because some transfers go to recipients outside the scope of the survey data collected by the Census Bureau and because recipients underreport, on average, the amount of transfer payments they receive. Therefore, the percentage reduction in the Gini index attributable to transfers probably understates the true magnitude of the effect.

[31] See Congressional Budget Office, *Unemployment Insurance in the Wake of the Recent Recession* (November 2012), www.cbo.gov/ publication/43734, and *Overview of the Supplemental Nutrition Assistance Program* (April 2012), www.cbo.gov/publication/43175.

[32]The percentage reduction in the Gini index attributable to government transfers and federal taxes is less than the sum of the percentage reductions resulting from each component. That occurs because the reduction stemming from federal taxes is calculated after the reduction resulting from government transfers.

End Notes for Appendix I

[1] CBO's reports on household income and taxation are posted together on the agency's website. See Congressional Budget Office, "Major Recurring Reports: Distribution of Household Income and Federal Taxes," www.cbo.gov/about/our-products/ RecurringReports#15. Supplemental data that present estimates for the 1979–2011 period are available at www.cbo.gov/ publication/49440.

[2] For this analysis, CBO considered refundable tax credits as negative income taxes rather than transfers. Federal taxes in this analysis were incurred in 2011 but not necessarily paid to the government in that year.

[3] That allocation reflects a consensus among economists. See Don Fullerton and Gilbert E. Metcalf, "Tax Incidence," in Alan J. Auerbach and Martin Feldstein, eds., *Handbook of Public Economics*, vol. 4 (Elsevier, 2002), pp. 1787–1872.

[4] For a more detailed discussion of CBO's methodology for allocating corporate taxes, see Congressional Budget Office, *The Distribution of Household Income and Federal Taxes, 2008 and 2009* (July 2012), www.cbo.gov/publication/43373.

[5] CBO measures capital gains income when realized, partly because estimates of accrued gains depend crucially on assumptions that are very uncertain and partly because maintaining consistency with the measurement of taxes (which are levied on realized gains) is valuable. Various researchers have measured capital gains as they accrue, on the basis of assets held by households at different income levels; those researchers have reached disparate conclusions about the effect of accrued capital gains on levels and trends in income inequality, depending in large part on their assumptions about the rate of return on assets. See, for example, Timothy M. Smeeding and Jeffrey P. Thompson, "Recent Trends in Income Inequality," in Herwig Immervoll, Andreas Peichl, and Konstantinos Tatsiramos, eds.,*Who Loses in the Downturn? Economic Crisis, Employment, and Income Distribution,* vol. 32 (Research in Labor Economics), pp.1–50, http://tinyurl.com/qdk92x4; and Philip Armour, Richard V. Burkhauser, and Jeff Larrimore, *Levels and Trends in United States Income and Its Distribution: A Crosswalk From Market Income Towards a Comprehensive Haig-Simons Income Approach*, Working Paper 19110 (National Bureau of Economic Research, June 2013), www.nber.org/papers/w19110.

[6] Most of the income in this category is pension income. That income includes taxable annuity payments from defined benefit pension plans; taxable withdrawals from defined contribution plans, such as 401(k)s; and taxable withdrawals from individual retirement accounts.

[7] Health care benefits are measured using the Census Bureau's estimates of the average cost to the government of providing those benefits. For more details on CBO's approach to valuing health care benefits and the consequences of that approach, see Congressional Budget Office, *The Distribution of Household Income and Federal Taxes, 2008 and 2009* (July 2012), www.cbo.gov/publication/43373.

[8] Income measured over several years is more equally distributed— although only modestly so— than income for a single year. See Congressional Budget Office, *Effective Tax Rates: Comparing Annual and Multiyear Measures* (January 2005), www.cbo.gov/publication/16212.

[9] That adjustment implies that each additional person increases a household's needs but does so at a decreasing rate. For example, a household consisting of a married couple with two children and an income of $80,000 would have an adjusted income of $40,000 ($80,000/'14) and would have the equivalent economic ranking of a single person with an income of $40,000 or of a childless married couple with an income of $56,600 ($56,600/'12 is almost $40,000). See Constance F. Citro and Robert T. Michael, eds., *Measuring Poverty: A New Approach* (National Research Council, 1995), http://tinyurl.com/mdhqjb4.

INDEX

D

E

F

G

H

I

K

L

M

S

T

U

V

W

Y